The Other New York

A Story About Human Transformation

By Bruce Richard

The Other New York:

A Story About Human Transformation

A story about an employee workforce in the 1980s who confronted their own demons to transform their workplace.

Copyright 2015 by Bruce Richard

All rights reserved. This book or any portion thereof may not be reproduced or used in any manner whatsoever without the express written permission of the publisher except for the use of brief quotations in a book review or scholarly journal.

First printing: 2015

ISBN: 978-1-329-48180-0

Bruce Richard

90 Cornell St. #2591

Kingston, NY 12402

brucerichardbook@gmail.com

Dedication

I dedicate this book to my former co-workers, whose work with one another diverted a river away from drowning hopes and dreams, emancipating us to soar high in the sky, and on whose wings I continue to ride.

The Other New York:

A Story of Human Transformation

Table of Contents

Forward 7

Introduction 9

Chapter 1: Competing Against Ourselves 17

Chapter 2: Finding Each Other 27

Chapter 3: Discovering Our Worth 43

Chapter 4: Who Are We to Transform 63

Chapter 5: Uncovering Mysteries Together 79

Chapter 6: Controlling Our Work 101

Chapter 7: We Can't Do It Alone 115

Chapter 8: Fighting For Our Lives 133

Chapter 9: Beyond the Storm 145

Acknowledgements 159

Forward

By Harry Belafonte

Think about it for a few moments: Combine a day-to-day life of hard physical work with little income, constant disrespect, racial issues and the uncertainty of young employees entering public life. For many it may be a formula of insurmountable obstacles. However, a little push here and there from the institutions in our society can allow the work environment and social relations to end up with far different outcomes.

This story is about how swiftly change can occur, and reminds us that though we may find ourselves in predicaments prompted by injustice, we have the primary responsibility to address how we work among ourselves to be able to successfully leverage our demands.

Bruce Richard, an Executive Vice President for 1199 SEIU, United Healthcare Workers East, presents us with how he faced this dangerous formula 30 years ago, along with a New York City workforce, mostly Latino and Black in their early 20s. They were taking their first job and naively expecting that their employer would have some real sense of obligation about their welfare. Then they hoped the city of New York, which was benefiting from the contracting out nature of their work, collecting the money from the city's parking meters, would correct working conditions unworthy to the job.

In my own life, I learned about widespread institutional racism in New York, and I too was kicked around in various jobs.

Our institutions--our workplaces, schools, city institutions-- all can do more to advance social progress.

Read this book and ask yourself: Did it have to be this hard for these young men to find their way?

This story, while tragic, is also an upbeat lesson to those invisible souls, least seen and recognized in our society, struggling to improve their lives. It's about what happened in New York City at a time when corruption was too easy a choice. But also puts the spotlight on our everyday, young workforce of the future, who had to find something more important than individual greed, whether for money or power.

Their story is a case study of how a workforce plays a vital role in steering us through daily labor/management problems, and the basic need for all of us to seek dignity in work, no matter what.

Enjoy.

Introduction

Even before dawn, I get up quietly so as not to disturb my wife, and like clockwork, find space on the floor for stretches to loosen up for the day. I put on the worn out blue trousers and the blue shirt with a wide orange stripe provided by the company, and drive to work in the dark. It is still before 6 a.m. when I arrive, along with perhaps one other early bird. We are on a rooftop parking area atop a former shopping center a block long. We might greet one another and take stock of whatever the previous day left behind and hints of what weather we face before rushing off to get our vehicles on the other end of the parking area.

I open the van door, and as always, hear the loud squeak, like the scream of a black bird in anger or pain, that comes with the vehicle. Almost before I know it, I'm in the driver's seat of this broken vehicle that will carry us to collect the money from New York City's parking meters. I turn the engine key, and after lots of spits and sputters, the van is running. It occurs to me – again -- that these vehicles will never be upgraded. There is no heat or air conditioning, just a fan blowing air, and sounds that synchronize the daily rattles of shabbiness and coins into an orchestra that performs in sync with the AM radio 1600 oldies station, and with the squeals of near-bald tires that notice every bump along the way. The brakes scream out, emitting odors; the van operates sluggishly. It all will indicate that we will be carrying more weight in coins than the vehicle is designed to hold.

Three or four of us occupy the two seats and whatever we can find for seats. Our décor changes as we locate crates and furniture in the streets to use as seats. Of course, it is very dirty inside the vehicle; filth has accumulated in crevices from everyday spills. The windows are smutty from rain or sleet, and there is a film on the inside that may conceal the daily fear we feel each day. I have managed to clear a window space to navigate. I race to be the first to get to the loading dock. The sooner I get out with my crew, the sooner I am back and my day is done.

There are many other businesses with large electronic garage doors lined up near us. This is the location not only for my company, the contractor Cosmopolitan Care Corp., but also for the city Department of Transportation, which is separated by a conveyor belt that sends us our equipment every day and receives the revenue.

It is all routine. I am given the names of collectors assigned to my vehicle, as well as the areas where we will collect. Keys to the meters are delivered by a conveyor belt in what looks like a red toolbox with numerous cables for each collection area. Each cable can have as many as 100 keys and some cables can have as few as 20-30 keys on the cable. The equipment has to be counted to make sure everything corresponds. We load the van with the canisters for the coins, the cable boxes with the keys and the carts used to carry the canisters. You have to inspect the cart first because many are broken, held together in makeshift ways, and you don't want to make matters worse by damaging it further; there are not enough good ones to go around.

We head for the first collection area, grabbing something to eat along the way. Today it is Brooklyn. The only semblance of security is the two-way radio that each van carries to announce the beginning and end of each collection area. On the way, the fear sets in. Everyone appears to handle it differently. For me, it's the feeling you get just before a fight that you are determined to win. You can hear the sound of collectors adjusting the various wraps for their legs, back and arms, wrapping their fingers with surgical tape and putting gloves on. It's the moment where our crew parachutes into uncertainty.

To the extent we work together, it's because we must. We don't trust each other and we are always trying to get a leg up on the other, craving for more than the next person. We are all facing the same monster, and yet we seem to suffer separately. The greatest way we work in cooperation is through our frequent thefts from the meters.

Collectors will walk 10 miles today, pulling rickety carts holding coins that will weigh over a hundred pounds. Each collector will turn the key of hundreds of meters every day. Injuries will be common. We must jump out of the van enthusiastically every day, showing confidence, never giving the slightest indication that anything is wrong, never giving anyone an opportunity to take advantage. Each guy grabs a chain and snaps it onto his belt, moving to their first meter.

Wop-wop-wssh-waam. You hear the rhythmic sound meter after meter, while the crew constantly exchanges canisters and cables of keys through the various ethnic communities of the city. By the end of today, we will ride back to the base in silence, most with eyes closed, resting and wondering how this life can be a stepping-stone. As always, we will each think quietly and plan individually, never trusting each other, totally exhausted.

* * *

It was New York City in the early 1980s, a time when urban mean streets turned really ugly with crime, drugs and lack of money for services, when headlines said New York City could drop dead. It was a time that news organizations and history books describe New York City as a cauldron for corruption in public government, and it was a time when crack cocaine made its arrival on streets turned unsafe for workers. We saw it all from a unique, inexperienced perspective as Parking Meter Collectors for a city that wanted the revenues we collected, but that did not know how to recognize the burdens it had created for us.

We Parking Meter Collectors had the audacity or just blind hope to think that we could solicit basic compassion to protect our bruised bodies, to correct decrepit working conditions and to treat us fairly. We were carrying tens of thousands of dollars in change through those streets, fearing for our lives in a very real way, and forcing ourselves to overcome obstacles that historically have often been unachievable by society's cheapest workers.

We saw ourselves as true believers in the American Dream; it was probably truer that we were like a flock of chickens that did not know that the fox existed. We thought the injustice was so obvious, and there were gatekeepers somewhere out there to protect us. We felt we only needed to expose the problem, and the system would intervene and correct it, and we could make these jobs our future.

We were all mostly young adults at our very first real job, not yet cynical. We were hired when New York City contracted out our services to the lowest bidder, who, in turn, found the most inexpensive labor to tolerate the least adequate work conditions. It was all part of a carefully orchestrated business plan, since parking meters brought the city as much as $60- to $80-million dollars annually. Ten years earlier, parking meter collectors had comprised an all-white workforce of city workers receiving wages three times our $5-an-hour rate. Then, there were twice as many employees performing half the amount of work, using safe and secure vehicles.

The arrival of crack cocaine to the scene created an environment immediately more threatening for us. Simply put, we were targets as we carried as much as $34,000 in change every day per truck. We were in dilapidated vehicles, with no protection, very little supervision, dragging faulty equipment that weighed well over a hundred pounds. All the while, there was the temptation to take some of the money. We saw it among fellow workers. Money disappeared between collection and delivery, along with the daily challenge to resist corruption itching to permanently scar our souls.

Our story happened at a time of what many have described as unparalleled corruption in New York City government. During this period, much of the city's administration resigned or was ousted, and there were reports of suspicious deaths of Donald Manes, the Queens Borough president, and union officials with whom we had dealings. Indeed, over time, we came to believe that we knew the deal and could recognize or even witness the shenanigans going down around parking meter collection. We understood all too well that a part of our role was to end up as scapegoats with damaged characters and reputations for any collection shortfalls.

The parking meter collectors were prey for a predator city in crisis. We needed assistance and naively reached out for help from union leaders who proved oblivious to our needs and who found themselves involved in pressures from organized crime bosses. Indeed, our union president and secretary treasurer were found bound, gagged and shot multiple times in the union headquarters.

Only eventually did we parking meter collectors realize that it was critical that we develop trust and confidence in each other as a first line of defense. Like most serious puzzles, it took a long effort to learn to conduct ourselves better, to overcome distrust and stealing, to discover that our work was valuable and that we could improve our working conditions.

One morning we formed a circle, held one another's hands, bowed our heads, and vowed to never steal from each other or the meters again. We promised to treat each other and the public we served with respect. We decided that we were worthy human beings, entitled to a decent life in exchanged for the hard work that we performed for the people of New York. We became the "New York City Parking Meter Collectors," no longer simply "the guys that got the money out of the parking meters". We sidestepped the assault on our dignity.

Looking back, what became obvious to we parking meter collectors was the fact that working people can be catalysts of immense social significance. We had found ourselves adrift in a system that was bent on keeping us down and at one another. One would think that there could be a workforce strategy somewhere in all of what we went through that rather could give voice to working people. This matter represents one of the nation's Achilles' heels.

This story is about a two-year campaign in which we struggled with our employer, the union leadership, the City of New York, and ourselves. We were eager young men, who ultimately just wanted to be proud participants among working people, to make our contribution to our city and create a decent life for our families and ourselves.

The system — legal, political, financial -- at almost every critical point opted to preserve the corporate right of employers to have absolute control over its workforce. Virtually all of the city administrative doors we knocked on were closed in our faces, as we were told they were neutral when it came to labor disputes, and city officials changed the rules when it suited them so that our actions would not inconvenience our employer.

The commitment was demonstrated very clearly that in New York City you could run a business, employ cheap labor and have no fear of intervention. We learned firsthand that the laws are not neutral, they lean entirely too far in favor of corporate interest, empowering them at the expense of social progress. We tolerate the reality of there being so many human beings needing work for whatever the employer will pay, vulnerable and set up to be economically and socially molested. This is the unfortunate predicament that many working people find themselves in today. It is the quality of the labor/management relationship that allows us to check the pulse of society's maturity. The workplace is more than a location where work is performed and business transpires. The workplace is also a location of major social importance.

It's in the work environment among ourselves that we were able to shake off internalized negative images of each other and ourselves as being worthless, unintelligent Latinos and Blacks, which placed ourselves in a better position to improve work outcomes. This empowering process is one that no one else can do for you. There are no short cuts. The groups' internal cohesiveness is what gives it viability.

In retrospect, it doesn't matter if you work in the West Virginia coal mines of Sago extracting coal or in a nursing home anywhere the elderly are simply warehoused, or if you are a recipient of homecare witnessing your experienced caregiver treated as disposable labor, or if you are an immigrant recruited to work in this country and exposed to the worst of stereotypes, or if you live in a working class community—like those adjacent to almost every metropolitan center—with an environment that is polluted and receiving questionable public services, and heaven help you if you are the victim of a hurricane! All of these are examples of how casually the value of human life is held beneath material preoccupation. Every working class ethnic group has experienced it. Every example of human abuse unfortunately injures society and makes it that much easier to tolerate the next example.

It is my hope that this document can be an illustration of why we must not allow ourselves to be sedated into believing there is some wise paternal gatekeeper out there to protect us. They are counting on us to walk away and expect someone else to take care of our problems. We must dedicate some portion of ourselves to overcome these critical challenges together, that we currently face separately.

Social transformation has been significant regarding gay rights, women's rights and racism. These arenas present us with vivid examples of social achievement. The work environment is also part of this social evolution, needing better balance between the employers and working people. However, unions largely have been marked by major decline over the last fifty years, finding the work environment more disconnected from the plight of communities where its membership resides and therefore not sufficiently linked to protect itself or its members. A critical symptom of the union decline is the deterioration of the employees' regard for each other. This has a dramatic impact on work outcomes, and for unions, this means that there is always more at stake than winning the employer fight: Unions have to place emphasis on liberating the fragile employee relationship. These circumstances have an impact on the production of goods and services, and necessitate fundamental changes from not only the employer but from the union. I am hopeful that this personal account can provide additional evidence to the reader as to where some shifts might occur.

The story of the New York City Parking Meter Collectors is about human beings that went from no trust and confidence in each other, to fully believing in each other and as a result achieving wonderful results. This document is also dedicated to all those that make the rescue of human spirit possible.

Chapter 1

Competing Against Ourselves

It all began for me on a very cold day: Nov. 31, 1984. Sixteen of us reported to a new job--collecting money from New York City's Parking Meters. We were sitting in the second floor room at the New York City Department of Transportation (DOT) building in Queens Village. Actually, we were to start working for Cosmopolitan Building Maintenance, a private company to which the city had outsourced this task, and today was the start of a newly won contract.

So here I was, sitting among the sixteen selected out of the hundreds that applied to Cosmopolitan Courier Corp. Wow, I thought: No more dodging taxis, trucks and buses on my bike as a messenger, no more carrying those heavy loads on my back, in the rain, cold and snow, I was so excited.

In an orientation session with two city transportation officials, we learned that Cosmopolitan had won the contract, but had no experience with parking meters. So they explained how the parking meters worked: We would carry cables with as many as a hundred keys that would open the meters, allowing us to remove a small coin box that released its coins into a canister. We would not see or touch the coins. We were told some coins had been marked or "salted" to assure that all the coins had been collected. If all the marked coins did not come back, it was assumed that whoever collected those meters stole money by breaking into the meter, the coin box or the canister. We were also told that the city or the company would follow us from time to time.

Our crews would include at least one driver for the van and one collector for each side of the street. The driver was supposed to stay in sight of both collectors. We would be issued uniforms, I.D. cards and a chain that will be connected to our belt to hold the keys on the cable – all mandatory. Drivers and collectors had to keep records of collections and broken meters.

After the orientation, John Masseo, a Cosmopolitan vice president, called eight names who would not be starting immediately. The other eight, including me, sat and waited, as a cold, terrorizing chill entered my body and a lot of angry people filed in. They were obviously very tired and worn out, many of them extremely dirty. A number of them had tape and bandages on their hands and fingers. They were the guys that were already working to collect money from parking meters from the company Cosmopolitan was replacing.

Most of them were Latinos in their early- to mid-twenties, a few were black; all of them were extremely upset. As Mr. Masseo brought them in, there were immediate questions in English and Spanish: How much money was he going to pay them? Mr. Masseo said he understood that many of them felt they had been getting a raw deal with the previous contractor, Armored Express, adding that Cosmopolitan was setting up a progressive wage increase system with a bonus system. He was interrupted again by the uproar. "Yo-man, how much money?"

Mr. Masseo said if you want this job, you'll be working for me and you'll call me Sir or Mr. Masseo. If not, get out. Everyone got silent. Any pretense I had of a professional atmosphere quickly disappeared. Now as I was saying, Masseo continued, I will be starting everyone off at $5 an hour. The uproar began again, someone saying, "You're cutting our pay," prompting several to leave the room. Mr. Masseo lost his calm composure, reddening. Listen, I'm not done, also we have this bonus system, he said. For those of you that are ready to work, well you'll be making a lot more money than you ever made with Armored Express. Our bookkeepers are still going over the exact details but a certain amount of meters will have to be collected, around 500, and after 500, each person will be paid ten cents per meter. The drivers will be given an amount that was equal to half the total after 500 meters. He said: I'll have all of this information in detail for you in the morning. There was silence, and then another worker spoke up saying that he hoped they were not playing games, and that Armored Express had not paid them for the last week's work. All were to report at 6 a.m. the following day except we eight new workers, who needed to start at 5:30 a.m.

I reported at 5:15 a.m. to begin my first day. I later learned that we would be getting paid starting from 6:30 a.m., but that we had to be present at 6. I was the first there, and it was still very cold. When everyone arrived, Mr. Masseo begins calling off the names of those designated to be collectors and those designated to be drivers. I was selected to be a driver and handed a route sheet for the day. Immediately there were some obvious looks and frowns from a number of faces, having to do with many of the collectors' disapproval of the decisions and the process, but everyone remained silent.

This would be the first time I had ever handled money. I was a little nervous but also still quite excited. I was assigned three collectors and a van. One of the collectors asked to see the route sheet and directed me to load the van with the proper canisters and keys. The van was badly dilapidated, with dents and damage, a window that did not work, a bumper section missing. They have an orange sign on each vehicle, indicating that they had been used to deliver newspapers in Orange County. There are not enough seats for everyone. One collector sat on a plastic crate, while the other two shared the passenger seat.

It was a rough start. We were all crowded into the van, with me driving. Everyone was angry about reduced wages and an unpredictable bonus system. My co-workers were also particularly upset with having to train the new people.

I drove to the lower east side of Manhattan, and it turned out that no one was familiar with the area to be collected. The two experienced collectors argued with one another about the route, while we newer two listened. The cold temperatures persisted, the collectors shivered. The new collector developed cuts and bruises on both hands from turning the keys of the meters; the veterans assured him that he would adjust, and showed hands with hardened calluses that have toughened from old bruises and cuts. I kept losing sight of the collectors, and had to keep driving around until I found them, often keeping them waiting. They would be standing on a corner with a look, holding the keys connected to their chain, a canister and all that money.

Even from the beginning, I felt upset that I could not keep track, and that anything could happen to them. I believed I was failing to do the job that I wanted so badly. Gradually, during the day, I did better. Surprisingly, only the new collector really complained. The veteran collectors treated the matter as a common occurrence and of no significance. We made it through the day. The new collector was thoroughly beat. He had walked close to 12 miles, pulling a heavy cart on wheels. It was late and took us twice as long since we did not know the areas and I did not know how to do the work.

Arriving back at the DOT, I saw several new guys holding and wrapping their bruised hands and moving in a hunched-over fashion. As the huge garage door gate opens for me to pull in to the site, I realized that I had been quite afraid all day. As I backed the van into the loading dock, I also was unloading a heavy responsibility: all that money in the van and no protection. We pulled the canisters out, and other designated people checked the haul. So my first day has ended, 13 hours later, I was told that we collected a small load of money today and it will be getting heavier. I took my tired self home and went straight to bed exhausted in ways I never had experienced before as a bicycle messenger.

The next morning I was into work early. I met Chapman, the newly appointed supervisor. He had been a collector and driver for the previous contractors, and he promised to smooth the operation by assigning collectors and drivers to more familiar routes. As workers arrived, talk turned to the bonus system. Mr. Masseo said hurriedly that whoever collected the most meters got the most money after the first 500, ten cents each meter after that. We headed out to our areas; I was assigned a Queens route this time.

On the way, Gil, an experienced collector, started giving me a hard time; he told me he wanted to drive, and then that he wanted the cables with the most keys in hopes of making the most money. The collectors began to bicker over who would have what cables. I attempted to intervene, but with little success. It was as if we were in a pit of rattlesnakes. As driver, I was supposed to be in charge, but because the collectors knew the areas, they were really in charge and gave me direction.

As I had been instructed, I dropped off two collectors in one area and went to drop the third in a parking lot. I then returned to exchange the cables of the two collectors. I followed them until they finished, exchanging cables one more time. Gil finished first and joined me to exchange the cable in the parking lot. When we arrived, we both observed the collector, who appears to be startled, throwing a big handful of quarters under a parked car. Gil told me not to say a thing, that he would report it, but I told the collector that I would have to report the incident. He said that the quarters had been stuck on top of the coin box and that he dropped them.

I really did not want to be involved, it being my second day, and the possibility existed of getting someone fired for theft. But I also did not want any confusion with my co-workers. I reported in to base by phone every hour and said there had been an incident; Chapman took the report and came out to our location, accepting the collector's explanation. We continued to fight among ourselves over who would collect the most meters. Collectors would be rushing to the rear of the van trying to get their hands into the cable box first so that each could try to get the cable with the most keys. Because the collectors knew the areas, we finished quicker, even though we collected a lot more meters, and again ended the day quite exhausted.

The days that followed were much the same, fighting and arguing among ourselves over keys and possible bonuses, heavy work and incidents of obvious theft. I could not leave anything unwatched. Sneakers and coats, pads and pencils were stolen. Someone was always searching through the vans and loading dock for items to take. Conversation was mean, and we were competing for money. There were drugs and alcohol in use. A number of the guys went to the same church and bring back talk of backstabbing and cheating wives. In short we were a mess.

We were locked into our separate lives, desperate for any semblance of achievement. Gaining advantages over the other person seemed to be the main measure of success to give us validation as praiseworthy human beings.

Our relationship with the public was unbelievably bad. We were shouting out the window, cracking jokes and insults to the public, and we were whistling and making degrading remarks to women. Cosmopolitan provided lockers and mandatory uniforms, but these were second-hand clothing with worn pants and shirts with an orange prison-like stripe across the front and jackets with holes in them. Honestly, we looked quite bad out in public.

After a few weeks, each vehicle was equipped with a two-way radio and we were required to call in at the beginning and end of each area. Everyone had to wear the uniform, an ID card and a chain for the cable of keys, which had to be attached to the collector's belt. For security purposes, collectors were rotated from van to van and drivers were never to work with the same collectors two days in a row.

I met enough people to know that everyone was unhappy. I would hear a lot of the usual ethnic rivalry with workers looking out for their own group, and when it comes to even their group they stood alone. Most of the guys were Latino; most were married with children and between the ages of 22 and 27. No one had been able to last longer than five years.

Because we were out in the street with money with no visible back-up, fear had a way of sneaking up. Especially in the early evening, I found myself starting to drive fast all the time. You have to be fast to locate a collector, I believed. I felt wild. I did not want anything to happen to the collectors who were with me; they were carrying around with them over a thousand dollars in a single canister. Collectors had to be tough in those streets. People would come up making all kinds of comments, sometimes annoying, sometimes threatening to take the money. A collector had to know how to handle these situations.

You could hear a *wop-wop-wsssh-waam* noise from the collection process at the meters and an occasional loud scream; *Baya!* It was amazing to see these collectors go so fast pulling that entire heavy load. The public moved quickly out of the way. Sometimes a collector was so fast in a race that he would leave the other collector many blocks behind. Often at the end of a long race you could find the winner in the van for a while, all done while others were still out collecting.

It was a really bad feeling to lose a collector. I drove like a madman in search of my co-workers, thankful upon locating him. It was in this way that we all could share common ground. Our behinds were all on the line, together we were sitting ducks, but yet we had this dislike, instigated by the employer, that pit us against each other.

* * *

Finally came that first payday. Everyone had bills to pay that have fallen behind. Once again, I was the first at work, and on this day, we got out and back early, only to learn that our paychecks would not be there for another few hours. Needless to say, the crews were upset. Finally the paychecks arrived, but

Chapman informed us that the bonus had not been included. I don't think I have ever seen an angrier group. Everyone retrieved their paychecks and went their way. This was a very powerful anger.

On Monday we were told that our bonus would be included in our next paycheck. Morale was rock bottom. We all dragged ourselves through the routes. Often the collectors would have to stop, jump back in the van, huddle around the heater attempting to bring some life back into their hands, fingers and feet. Like many of the vans, my van did not have a heater that generated enough heat.

I started going out collecting, and letting one of the collectors drive. My fingers first got cold, then numb and then they hurt from the metal keys as I went from meter to meter. The keys bruised my fingers in the turning process of the meters, until hundreds had been done. My hands were bleeding, fingers blistered and raw, my entire body numb. But after a couple of weeks the calluses helped. My co-workers appreciated seeing me make the effort to collect the meters. There was often talk about lazy drivers.

We were not expected to take a real lunch break, and there was nowhere to use the restroom. Imagine owning a bar or restaurant and you see a raggedy, filthy man come in and ask to use the restroom. We had to improvise. We would pull alongside a parked vehicle to relieve ourselves in an artful way. No one seemed to notice. Pizza was the most common diet; we would grab it real quick in route to the next area. You did not want to be in one place too long with all that money.

Behind the van's two seats were canisters with the retrieved coins. Every time we hit the brakes, the canisters shifted, occasionally hitting someone. Workers also complained about grease that the maintenance group used on the meters. It got all over our clothing and stung the skin and eyes. Our hands hurt, the canisters were heavy, the carts to haul the canisters had faulty wheels. By Friday, bodies ached all over.

Next week, the paychecks were late again. But worse, once they arrived, the guys started opening their checks and cursing aloud over the smallness of the promised bonus. I looked at my paycheck; it was painful. I felt trapped like a fly on sticky paper; I have been fooled. I have not really escaped the fate and danger of being a bike messenger. I realize I have really been lured into a greater danger, a greater fear and still with my life on the line. I went home for a weekend that would see very little Christmas shopping.

It was Christmas Eve, cold as ever. I was loading my van when Robles, one of the Bronx boys, says: "Hey don't load up, we ain't goin' out. We're meeting outside on the loading dock." I left my load unfinished and joined my co-workers outside. Most of the guys were there, and nervous energy was obvious. There was mounting uncertainty about what to do, but restlessness over the fact that something had to be done. Robles spoke up, but there was no plan, and arguments started to break out. I was a bit shook up because we could be fired if we returned from a visible meeting like this with no togetherness. Some of us could be singled out and made examples of.

I quickly spoke before anyone could leave: "Hey we can't leave, let's talk. We are in serious hot water." My throat was tight and it was quite difficult attempting to speak up for the first time. I had been a part of social justice activities in my community in the past, but I had never been a person who addressed a crowd or a dispute on the job. I needed a job just as much as the next person but something had to be done and we were the only ones to do something. "We have to quit arguing among ourselves. He is treating us like shit, while we have just walked off the job together and are arguing with each other," everyone agreed. Felix Aponte nodded his head. I respected this young brother very much and so did others. "We should demand an end to the bonus system and request a raise in pay," someone shouted. Jose Aponte spoke up; "we took shit with all these companies," he said. "We took shit with CDC, We took shit with Armored Express, and this has got to stop. We haven't even got our last weeks pay from Armored Express." Eddie Montalvo said, "You guys know I have three kids and I'm having a hard time with this cut in pay." We all agreed that nine dollars an hour would be fair.

Mr. Masseo was standing on the dock and we approached him as a group. Robles said, "we are all upset over the way we are being treated, it's not fair. This treatment cannot continue and the guys want nine dollars an hour." Masseo appeared sympathetic, saying that he thought the bonus system could be improved, and that he would consider our proposal if we would load up our vehicles and began work.

In the following days in my overcrowded vehicle, we rehashed our brief work stoppage, the first meeting among ourselves. I was starting to feel a slight connection to these guys. I was hearing comments about who was with us and who was not. I remained quiet and cautious. I wondered in what direction our concerns could move. There were all kinds of opinions, but no information. The week vanished rapidly; Mr. Masseo never got back to us to respond to our discontent.

On the next payday, two collectors were with me, Eli and Felix. They were fast on the route. All you could hear was the repeated *wop-wop-wssh-waam* as they flew up the streets and side blocks from meter to meter. This was clearly an art that many of the collectors have learned well, through cold, sleet or storm it didn't matter. This Friday Eli won by half a block. We finished our job early this Friday, but again there were no paychecks before 8 p.m.

I was troubled over the situation. Mr. Masseo demonstrated absolutely no respect towards us. The wear and tear on me, carrying all this money with no security or protection was quite problematic. Unfortunately, we were very much in disarray and confused over what to do about these conditions.

Chapter 2

Finding Each Other

I reported to work on Monday morning; it was New Year's Eve, but among the early arrivals, there was no sense of holiday. Nature's early morning temper of cold preferred to leave a lasting impression concerning this particular last day of the year.

On the loading dock, we were just starting to load our vehicles when someone shouted: "We're not working! Hell no! Let's go outside." So we went outside, leaving Chapman, the supervisor, confused.

Within moments, we were having an impromptu, unauthorized work meeting. We decide that Jose Aponte, Eddie Montalvo and I should take one of the vans and go to the U.S. Department of Labor or to anyone that has some authority to do something about what was going on here. We believed government would not allow bad working conditions and problems with pay to continue. We agreed that everyone else would not start work until the three of us returned. We sounded much like a football team coming out of a huddle.

So the three of us took off, only to have to pull over at a pay phone to learn where we were headed; the Department of Labor was in lower Manhattan. It should have been a sign -- as a workforce, we don't know where we were going either, other than the fact that we have launched ourselves towards a fix for our problems. Of course, we got to the Labor Department only to learn that on New Year's Eve, there would be few people there. Nevertheless, a receptionist helped us find an official, who told us that it was the National Labor Relations Board that we should see.

We would follow all helpful advice, we said. Considering that we had some hope that these issues might get resolved today, we were now starting to wonder. We have just told the Department of Labor what we believe was earth-shaking information and no alarm went off or gotten even a comment. We had this expectation that we would explain to an authority about all this money we carry around for the city and how we were exposed and unprotected, and they would put the employer on notice, have an investigation and remedy the situation right away. We had made an erroneous assumption, but we did not know what to expect.

The National Labor Relations Board (NLRB) also was open, though it looked like a ghost town. The official we met had us fill out complaint forms, adding that he normally did not offer advice, but that it sounded as if we needed the help of a union. He recommended that we check out District 65, a transportation workers' union. They may be just the union for us, he said. He explained that the country was not in a labor-friendly mood, and that the NLRB had lost budget and staff.

We were given copies of the complaints we filed. Not entirely disappointed, we had accomplished a couple of things. We had a lead to a possibly good union and we have filed complaints. We certainly had learned a lot. We had thought the Labor Department was an agency that existed to serve the needs of working people needing help. We now questioned if any such government agency even existed, outside of their labor-friendly-sounding names. How does one get information about these kinds of things? I should have learned in school about all my rights as a working person, it should have been a mandatory subject. I asked myself and my co-workers repeatedly why this does not exist.

So asking for help was creating more work for us to find help. Any expectation that the agencies would offer immediate relief in correcting our problems was misplaced; it seemed as though we did not understand where the line was drawn regarding corporate influence.

By the time we got back to the DOT, we learned that Channel 7 News had been called and had come by to interview us about our complaints, including reports of injuries on the job. The energy level on the loading dock was very high among my coworkers.

In a panic, a number of the guys also had been speaking with the street vendors and small businesses on Metropolitan Boulevard and calling friends and family for advice, implementing whatever they individually thought made sense, with little communication and coordination with each other. Eddie had already called District 65 from a phone booth and made arrangements for a meeting.

Management, meanwhile, was extremely upset by the possibility of being fined because we had not yet collected the meters. Daily fines could be $35,000, but all of us had stood our ground since 6 a.m. and not one vehicle had gone out.

Mr. Masseo stood on the dock with his hands on his hips, cigar in his mouth and chest out, looking very angry and pleading for us to start work. We ignored him, and moved to the far end of the dock and decided that the important thing was for us to stick together. Otherwise, many of us would be fired and working conditions would remain the same. We have just walked off the job for hours. Everyone had a look of worry over our faces. We were becoming more fearful than we were when we first walked out this morning.

Everyone looked different to me, their faces have changed and their height and stance seemed altered. You could tell Eddie was very concerned. This job was very important to him and his family. I was very concerned myself. It didn't seem as if any other moment could get more critical than this one.

One of the guys spoke up, saying that we should demand a wage increase. That was quickly echoed by everyone who said, "That's right, yeah, right." Then someone shouted that we should demand that we get some benefits and better protection as well, and that they not fire anybody who refused to work today. People really chimed in and agreed with that. Definitely we had to get them to agree not to fire us, to put it in writing. Someone else said, "Get them to agree to lighten our workload in these areas."

There was an air of determination. We wrote everything down on a clipboard, and sent me to outline the demands for Mr. Masseo. I wanted to say "not me," but couldn't. As we moved towards him, Mr. Masseo shouted, "Oh, what do we have here? A Puerto Rican standoff?" and laughed, adding "yeah, I'm Italian." As I started listing the demands, he interrupted, shouting, "I will give an additional $50 to whoever will go out and collect the meters, right now." No response. Everyone stood silently. He then said, "Ok, so what are you saying?" I found the courage to read our demands: we want hourly wages increased to $10. He interrupted again to say, "That's more than the nine you had asked for earlier." I would not be distracted and continued: we want benefits and we want less work and greater safety for ourselves. I went on to say we want no repercussions against anybody that walked out this morning. He asked for a moment to confer with his management team.

In his absence, a great sigh went over the whole lot of us, and there was a lot of talk about the exchange, about unions, about the federal complaints against the employer with the National Labor Relations Board. We didn't really know what the significance of these charges would be, but the act proved useful to our morale.

Mr. Masseo came out waving his hands, offering to talk with our representatives. The three of us who had been selected earlier went inside and he said he knew we were in a difficult spot, that some of these guys were real troublemakers but that the three of us were decent employees. He said that if we stuck with him, we would go places and he would take care of us, make us supervisors. I was embarrassed and intimidated, and worried that he might be able to sway my team, which would mean sure defeat. There did not appear to be an honest bone in his body. I spoke quickly and in an innocent way, said that we were representing all the guys.

Mr. Masseo decided it to be a better tactic to be more straightforward and admitted that the vans were in terrible shape, and that he would try to get better vehicles within a couple of weeks. He said he would be willing to look anew at workloads and schedules. He asked what we think it would take to stop these illegal work stoppages. Jose told him that the guys were very angry and upset over cut wages, unsafe conditions and unsafe vehicles.

Agitated, Mr. Masseo said he was concerned over fines and that he wanted to postpone the talks. Mr. Masseo said the company would not pay $10, but would consider $8 an hour for drivers though less for collectors. We replied that we wanted everybody to be paid the same. He said, ok, I'm not totally sure but I think I can come close to $8 an hour for everyone. We told him, we needed to go outside and speak with the guys. Mr. Masseo got heated over how long this matter was taking and he insisted we hurry so we could collect the meters.

We went back to the guys to report. One worker said we wanted $10, not $8. Go back and tell them we wanted $12 or nothing--that we were not going back to work. Others shouted with agreement; we gave him our demands and if he wanted to mess around then we wanted $12. People had done this work 10 years ago and made as much as $16 an hour go tell him about that, they said. We went back and said that we wanted $14 an hour, angering Mr. Masseo. Impatiently, he agreed to pay $10 an hour—if people got moving now.

We quickly returned outside. "Did we have it in writing?" "Did we get an agreement that they wouldn't take any repercussions against us?" The questions continued. Realizing that we had not secured either of those things, we went back; Mr. Masseo said he agreed verbally, but that it was dependent on collections starting immediately, that we could have these statements in writing when collections were done in the evening. Despite reluctance, the guys agreed, and moved to load up trucks for a run that would run well into the evening.

No one felt that we had a victory, but clearly most of us were serious about the demand for things changing.

The day was already a cold one. It was below freezing and the wind was making it colder. All of us dreaded collecting meters late at night. We have been out there in the dark before, but this was definitely going to be the latest that we have ever been out collecting. I had two collectors with me, Foreman and Gonzales. I think both of them were among the few single men on the job, and among the youngest. They both really carried on in the van as the oldies music in the background was starting to make static. Our vehicle had very little heat. One window was broken; the back door was tied shut. We had lots of discussion about the ordeal we had just gone through together.

We arrived at our starting point on 86th Avenue where it was much colder because the wind was whipping off the ocean. After two hours, Gonzales and Foreman felt beat. After collecting a cable, they would jump into the van and huddle under the heater, both shivering, trying to warm their hands. When the sun went down it appeared as another world. Car lights danced off my eyes, the streetlights, the sky, the haze, constantly sparkled.

I drove slowly down the street; Foreman was on one side of the street and Gonzalez on the other. I started to lose sight of the collectors as they became further apart from each other. I didn't know where they were. They would turn down a side street. It was dark; I didn't know where they went. I was driving frantically up and down trying to locate them. I thought to go out myself and collect, but neither one of them had a driver's license, so I decided against it.

It was 9 p.m. and we still had a considerable amount of work ahead of us. I wondered how the company could justify putting us out here at night with all of this money. People would stop and look in disbelief; they were all dressed up on their way to a New Year's Eve celebration. What? You're getting the money out of the parking meters this late at night? Damn it's New Year's Eve!

I would pull alongside the collectors intentionally with my window down and my head hanging out in the cold, to share some of the agony they were feeling out there trying to turn those keys under dreadful circumstances. Trying to even locate the hole the key goes into had become a tremendous task and slowed us.

Finally, it was over. We were beat, shaken up and worn out. We headed back to the base at approximately 2 a.m. We were the second to the last van to get in. One was still out. We unloaded the van. The operation was deserted with only one supervisor. Of course, Chapman, showing his standard composure, was looking very alert. He had probably been there in some capacity the longest. He had been there with several contractors before, an African American, a seemingly fair person and a dedicated Jehovah's Witness. Chapman, looking sympathetic, half smiled and said, "Happy New Year."

* * *

New Year's Day was spent on the phone with a few of my co-workers. Everyone said that they had just gotten off the phone with another one of the guys. We were not about to get fired while we were sitting around doing nothing. We seemed to have a couple of things going for us--the charges we filed with the National Labor Relations Board and possibly District 65 representation. But these developments were not enough and we all knew it. I hoped we could hold it together among ourselves.

I felt an uneasy conflict within myself, being a little fearful about returning to work the next day. There was also a kind of excitement corresponding with this tremendous anxiety. Perhaps I should have been thinking about finding another job, maybe even going back to being a bicycle messenger. But there was this exciting attraction inside to let this play out. I felt so much more alive now. Underneath all of the turmoil and confusion among us, despite being upset about the stealing, drugs and disrespect, there actually was something I found appealing. I think it's called "progress."

We decided to meet in the parking area before work on the roof. We agreed again that we would not work unless we got the understanding we demanded from Mr. Masseo in writing. The meeting was chaotic with everyone trying to speak at once; once again, Eddie, Jose and I were appointed to confront management.

When we confronted him, Mr. Masseo pulled out his pen, grabbed a sheet of paper and wrote: "It's the intent of Cosmopolitan Care Corporation (Mr. John Masseo) to compensate its employees at an hourly wage of $10 per hour. This agreement will be in place and in effect until Cosmopolitan Care Corporation and its meter collector employees come to full agreement on a final wage and benefit settlement for employment at Cosmopolitan Meter Collection." He added a notary public stamp, but said he was only prepared to sign the wage offer.

I saw a look of relief across my coworkers' faces with Mr. Masseo having signed the agreement. It was also agreed that we would report to work at 6:30 am and have all the vehicles out by 7 a.m. We returned to the guys up in the parking lot with the agreement to pay everyone $10 signed and notarized. Everyone began to jump with joy. "All right!" "*Baya!*" Shouts of joy in English and Spanish, as we all went to load our vehicles. It felt a little unreal. I wondered if this could be just another trick and maybe I would still be fired, but that feeling was quickly suffocated by the pleasure of achievement around me.

We decided to meet for a noisy, joyful breakfast before going out to collect. Joining a union had become a big conversation; we all agreed we must have a union to legally protect ourselves.

We passed the word among ourselves that there would be a meeting with Bill Tate, a vice president at District 65, on the following Friday. We all knew we had to do something and quick. We all feared retaliation.

About sixty of us gathered at District 65 – one worker also inappropriately brought his girlfriend -- and told our tale. Bill Tate outlined the benefits and dues, and distributed union representation cards, adding after hearing our accounts that he was concerned for our safety. At one point, he let us know that he considered things to be so dangerous that he occasionally carried a firearm, which he showed us and let us know he understood our situation. As we left, there was an air of cooperation among the guys, a wonderful feeling.

* * *

The event of the day centered on Eddie Montalvo. We learned that Eddie had been appointed Chief of Operations. Eddie came in, threw up his arms, and said he hoped this would mean something for him and his family, though Mr. Masseo had not told him anything yet to finalize this. Jose told Eddie that he thought he needed to be careful about this position, and that Mr. Masseo may be trying to find a way to divide us. Eddie acknowledged that he has some of the same suspicions and was just waiting to see what this position involved.

We saw subtle changes. The number of cable boxes – the cables holding keys to meters – was increasing. And selected employees were taking vans home, with permission from Mr. Masseo, as long as they returned them on time for work. I guess there wasn't much concern about vans getting messed up, since they already were wrecks.

I was concerned about these developments. It occurred to me that this might be a divisive move by Mr. Masseo. I suspected that he was giving out favors to win loyalty from some of the guys. This way in which Mr. Masseo operated kept popping up as part of his routine. It appeared to be a weapon of some kind, which he used, that had the impact of pitting us against each other, and therefore pitted the people that need to have cooperation around the work, against each other. I did not think he intentionally wanted to pit us against each other; it seemed in his thinking to be his best option to get the work done, in a way that gave him control. But if we were divided, I did not think that helped him get the outcomes he wanted. I thought he needed employees who had the highest level of cooperation among themselves.

On Friday, we learned that our $10 an hour wage was not reflected in our paychecks.

We met again with Bill Tate of District 65, only to learn that because of some AFL-CIO jurisdiction issues, it appeared that we come under the jurisdiction of the International Longshoreman's Association, Local 1964 rather than District 65. He introduced us to Pablo from the ILA. None of us objected. We trusted Mr. Tate's judgment. So we gave signed new union representation cards to Pablo, who said that the ILA had some familiarity with our employer, which surprised us. He said they might approach the employer with the cards showing they have a majority, and give the employer a chance to voluntarily recognize the union, avoiding a representation election. Pablo said the ILA maintained a small local in New Jersey, with a great deal of influence. He thought the ILA could get Cosmo to agree to fair and decent terms, which was really what we wanted to hear.

On the following day, Pablo and Richie, another union staff person, joined us on the loading dock after working hours. Pablo had a big smile on his face. He said, "Congratulations. You are all now members of the ILA, Local 1964." He said the employer obviously didn't want any trouble; you guys have done a fine job. It appears the employer really wants to cooperate and has agreed to sit down and negotiate a contract. Pablo said; keep up the good work, stay cool and try not to have a lot of friction right now as that might prevent us from getting a good and rapid agreement from the employer. We will take care of this employer. You guys don't worry, just do your jobs and give me a call if you're having any problems.

The word flew quickly of us being in the union and reached every parking meter collectors ear in an effortless motion. Having achieved this within two months really inspired some of us.

However we learned that Mr. Masseo had been talking with some of the guys, threatening to lay them off, claiming he could not pay them the agreed-on wages. But if they would agree to $5 an hour until the finances picked up, he will keep them on. He got a few people to actually sign papers agreeing to be paid $5 per hour. A couple of the guys said they didn't have a choice: They were either going to sign the papers or be sent home.

Everyone was informed that we were now members of the union, which we were very excited about. "Great. Now they can get busy on some of these problems we're having with Mr. Masseo." So we called Pablo, the union representative, and told him what was going on. He told us not to worry. They were planning a big meeting with us and we would also discuss the terms we want in the agreement with Cosmopolitan.

Meanwhile there was yet another new development: Everyday, new people showed up to work. A number were sent home because there was no work for them. There was no seniority. There just was a list of people who will be called upon when needed, but they all had to report to work every day. We now were seeing a large number of people showing up every day competing for work. Since there were so many on the job injuries, a number of these people got work.

These new guys were inexperienced so it was hard to work with them. Since I had only been around a short time, I needed direction from the more experienced collectors. In fact, I felt lost myself without an experienced collector.

So again we were working with four people to a vehicle, even though there were only two seats. Every time we hit the brakes, the canisters slid and sometimes flew around in the vehicle. My van's turning signals did not work, so I had to use hand signals, which made it difficult to keep the little heat in the vehicle.

This was a foolish plan on the part of Mr. Masseo. We were all slowed up, burdened with the responsibility of showing a lot of new people the job, most of whom will not last a day. He was going to get less from the workforce not more, and plus the quality of the work was going to be poorer. It was now more difficult for us to have the necessary cooperation among ourselves to get the job done effectively. Clearly Mr. Masseo was not paying attention to the right things.

Something else started to get my attention: We were stealing money from the meters. It was common to open a meter and have quarters just fall out on you, especially if there was no coin box in the meter. Sometimes a collector would take those quarters and keep them, and maybe take everyone to lunch. No one admitted that they were paying with quarters from the meters, but after a while you assumed it. I knew this was dangerous and I was complicit.

I got a message to call the Labor Relations Board agent. He wanted an update about what was going on, which we gave him. He thought that since the employer has recognized the union, we might want to withdraw the charges and try to get things worked out through the union. We had no problem with that.

We met again on the cold roof. One of the guys shouted, "The shop floor is now open." Everybody laughed about that and there was such a ruckus that it was difficult to have a meeting. We agreed that paychecks were still a problem; the checks were now on time, but not reflecting the promised $10 an hour rate. It was not clear why. We all began to speculate about this. Mr. Masseo told us he had not implemented the increase yet, and that they needed to do some major work on their equipment to input that change and they didn't have enough time to do it last week. One of the guys had asked Mr. Masseo when the electronic issue would be resolved, and Mr. Masseo had stated that since we were now members of this union, they would have to sit down and negotiate what our wages and terms would be.

The routes were very heavy. Cosmopolitan was trying to collect all the meters as often as they could. The company was getting approximately 44 cents for each meter being collected.

We worked diligently to do the work and to follow the advice of the union leadership. Mr. Masseo was getting very tough with us. He had no regard for the length of time that people were on the job and was sending people home in any way he wanted to, and that had the impact of terrorizing and creating fear.

Injuries were starting to multiply because of the workloads. There were a few people hit by canisters flying in the vans. There were reported injuries from pulling the heavy loads, crowded conditions in the vans, long hours and safety problems. We were starting to drop like flies.

Pena was one of the collectors with me; he was injured and having a hard time keeping up. His hand was swollen and halfway down his index finger was a bad blister that has gotten infected and was bleeding, and being agitated every time he attempted to turn the key at the meter. He tried to double the gloves on that hand, but it did not work. He was barely able to get through the day. After that, I insisted that anyone who was injured should not go out.

We continued to meet briefly in the parking area, which was cold in the early mornings. The wind was singing an unpleasant song on the roof, slicing through our worn uniforms. The glimpse of the stars and the moon seemed to indicate that magnificence could prevail through difficulty.

The guys were in agreement about an injury policy, but that was one of a number issues facing us. One of the guys said a friend of his told him our union was run by the Mob. Discussion went all over the place and there was no agreement if this information helped or harmed us, and at this point, it was only what one of the guys said. We agreed to get more information. However, the shades of right and wrong about the Mob statement were absolutely blurred by our desperation.

People were complaining that Cosmopolitan was doing whatever they want to do. They were sending long-term workers home, working us too hard and failing to implement the pay increase. Guys were saying we stuck our necks out, hoping to get someone to fix our problems, and so far we haven't gotten anything in return. As we went about our daily work, it was unclear what we have gotten ourselves into. In addition, we were stealing and showing disrespect among ourselves and with the public. Things seemed pretty bleak.

It was common for us to pull up to a parking meter to start our day, and when a woman walked by, we would jump out of our dilapidated vehicle with our raggedy, torn uniforms, shouting to women, "Ay, Mommy. Hey, baby, come here. You got the time, I got the place," and on and on and on. We were notorious for disrespecting people. Taken as a whole, we don't demonstrate any respect for the public, don't show any respect for each other and don't have any respect for ourselves.

One day, when I was using a pen and paper to record the cable box count, I set the pen down. When I returned, the pen was gone. I was upset, and even more so when I located my pen in the hand of this new guy. I knew he and a couple of other guys came to work every day and went through the vans searching for things they wanted.

I was trying to help us keep it together and I did not think there was a chance in hell for me to keep this job unless we stood together. Masseo would have a few of us out of here and quick.

There was absolutely no way that you could work here and not be complicit or directly involved in the theft. Others said they would give me a cut of the money when we went out together. I had to persistently say I was not interested, as the requests were repeated frequently.

Two weeks went by and we still had not heard back from the union leadership. Cosmopolitan was on the offensive and doing whatever they want, and never once asking us what we think about anything. It was clear that something had to be done.

Meanwhile, two collectors were discovered to have been stealing money from the meters and were fired. One of the guys was the same person whom I saw on my second day out stealing, and tossing quarters under a parked car after being startled by us.

The problem was we could not see how theft was the option intentionally made available to us. It seemed as if we were expected to take this path. We got the crumbs illegally, and somebody else got the lion's share. It appears they were more than willing to have us be the ones in this role. However it was not the compensation that could really satisfy our needs.

It was starting to feel as though we were an object of some kind that someone might use to make money. When people look at us they think; "oh there's that object." "I need me a few of those objects to get my job done," "and of course you got to know how to maximize the use of the object, this is very important." It's a kind of legal theft of human beings. The even bigger problem was that many of us believed the same thing about ourselves and we positioned ourselves as an object so that a deal could be struck. It proved to be a form of job security.

Chapter 3

Discovering Our Worth

We decided one morning that we could wait no longer on the union leadership and that we would have to act ourselves to get the word out to different community groups and organizations. We realize we need help with the thinking; entirely too much was coming at us all at once. So we met again on the roof in another somewhat disorderly gathering. I was assigned to draft a letter. We agreed that the main pressure on our situation was from the city budget, and therefore should involve the Mayor.

For the first time, we described ourselves as the New York City Parking Meter Collectors, and we presented ourselves as having a significant role in the city with a real meaningful purpose and responsibility. It was like the ugly duckling story, where the ugly duckling eventually looks in the water, sees the reflection and discovers being a wonderful swan. We were really important for the city, though no one ever told us.

The letter outlined that the job of collection had been outsourced from city jobs to a contractor with the lowest bid, our horrible working conditions, and our unsatisfactory experience so far with the International Longshoremen Association local. We hinted we thought they might be a shady outfit. We described ourselves as mostly Latin, Black and people of color, and that race was responsible for much of our experience with the city and the contractor. We said that we were isolated and needed advice.

We circulated the draft among ourselves, and made changes to please our group. The whole notion of us being the New York City Parking Meter Collectors really started to take hold. The idea of us having an important role in the city had an impact. We were coming to grips with the fact that it was us and only us who brought in the money from all of the boroughs of New York City. But more importantly, we were making a statement about being in charge of our decisions. It was becoming apparent to many of us that we could not depend on anyone else to solve our problems. This letter memorialized our collective sense of responsibility.

Using the phone book, we pulled together a list of elected officials, community leaders and church ministers that we knew or had heard of. We wanted them to circulate our letter and explain it to any elected officials. We strongly believed that if the public knew what we were going through they would be concerned and these problems stopped.

Jose finally got through to Pablo just before the mailing went out. He said he was very busy, but that the union wanted to meet with us at 5 a.m. before work at a restaurant in Queens. This was unacceptable to us, said Jose, adding that we needed direction and action from our union leadership. So we started circulating our letter. The guys' imagination went wild with this 5 a.m. restaurant meeting proposal. One wanted to discuss something with me and took me to the trunk of his car and showed me several automatic weapons, AK 47s. I told him these would not be needed and that we could not win that way. It took no science to conclude that this direction would result only in the loss of our jobs, if not our lives. I felt a slight sense of something potent, an obvious product of my own deprivation.

Pablo then said the union would meet with a few of us, which we did, at a law office in downtown Manhattan. Pablo introduced Sol Bogon, a lawyer with a deep, tough, scratchy voice, whose first item was our letter to the public. Someone has sent it to them; I think to myself, oh shit. They did not appreciate the way they were being characterized in the letter. We listened particularly to one union official who did not introduce himself who said that the union had some idea about who is involved and that for us not to worry, they would take care of it. They connect the letter to some existing conflict with another party; it was all vague.

I told the union officials that I did not know whom you are talking about, but I drafted the letter from our guys on the job. I am trying to be somewhat apologetic for any problems the letter may have caused. Sol Bogon responded by saying: "who are you, why you're just a fly on the wall," and they acted in disbelief that I could have written such a letter and seemed to dismiss my words altogether.

Mr. Bogon gave us some ideas about what kind of agreement we could have. We told Mr. Bogon we wanted $10 per hour. He disagreed; "no way," he said. "No one is making $10 per hour for that kind of work." He went on to say that we had a decent employer with whom he has spoken and he thought that we could get a very good agreement, but not $10 per hour, this was unrealistic. He emphasized that we had to be realistic, that he had handled hundreds of contracts for guys doing similar kinds of work and nowhere were they making that kind of money. I wondered about his reference to guys doing similar kinds of work, was it similar geographically, similar racially, the meaning of this statement bothered me, since they have never represented parking meter employees as far as we know.

We told him we had a promise of $10 per hour in writing and notarized. He responded in disbelief and wanted to see it. We showed it to him, he scratched his head and said, "Well, it's here in writing, I don't know how real it is, but I'll look into it, but like I said this doesn't make a lot of sense." Eddie emphasized that we had to have the $10 rate. So we ended with a plan to have a bigger meeting with all the guys.

Everyone was eager to go to our first union meeting and meet the officials of the union. On the appointed day, everyone rushed out early to finish quickly to attend the meeting. Mr.

Masseo was in the loading dock as usual, making it clear that he did not care where we were going; he was in charge. He was flinging unnecessary orders about and being insulting, in terms of his "go here and go there" gestures.

All of us went to the meeting together on Metropolitan Boulevard at the American Legion Hall. The meeting room was poorly lit, and there was beer and refreshments, though no one took a beer. The atmosphere was quite stiff. There was Pablo, Richie, and Mr. Bogon, who took the lead in the meeting. He reviewed the fact that we had organized and been recognized by Cosmopolitan, adding that this meeting was specifically called so that we workers could make the union aware of additional issues that we would like in the contract. There were the now-familiar calls about health and safety, workload, pay, respect, seniority. Pablo and Richie appeared to be taking notes.

Sol Bogon said he had already been in touch with the employer, who seemed eager to reach a settlement. He knows we have the wage increase promise in writing indicating that Cosmopolitan would pay us $10 per hour. He said he thought this was a bit high, but, hey, they signed an agreement and we were going to do everything in our power to hold them to that agreement, and if they don't want to cooperate, the union will ram a bat up their ass. With that, there was a great deal of laughter, the guys really like that language. Bogon added that Jose Aponte and I would be appointed shop steward and assistant shop steward, which our guys liked. Mr. Bogon explained that we would begin paying dues, with deductions from our next paycheck, described the benefits, which were unclear, and apologized for any confusion about meetings. We were now feeling ourselves a part of an official organization. Everyone was excited. We then had a few beers and went home.

* * *

Often, after the snow melted a bit, there were large puddles of dark slush. The street had become a mixing bowl of debris and garbage, naturally blended together with the slush to produce these pockets with awfully deep puddles on the ground. It was common to a parking meter collector to be wading through these big puddles with his cart and canister, to get the money out of the meters. The guys were moving slowly and carefully from meter to meter trying to limit the amount of cold dirty slush from getting in our shoes. Once a collector's feet got wet, the cold feeling intensified and slowed up the work. We would often stop and buy socks when this happens. This problem always added to the already established difficulty of the day. It was because of this that we added the priority of boots to our list.

While our immediate working conditions had not changed, we had high expectations. We wanted these jobs to provide us with a future. For most of us, this was an effort to secure a stable long-term income, it was also the first time that most of us had ever come together as working people to achieve anything. When we got together, sometimes the atmosphere would resemble strength. And so there was reason for optimism.

At our next rooftop meeting we decided that it was too cold and difficult to continue to meet on the roof every morning, and we took ourselves down into the building, located a room and started our meeting. Mr. Masseo was not there, but the supervisor looked up and ignored us, and so, we held our discussion. Jose started to take control of the meeting, demanding that there be no more talking all at once, and that everyone had to raise a hand to be acknowledged before speaking. It was agreed.

There was also a dynamic in all the meetings where there was the necessity for English translation. The people who did not speak or understand English very well always stood in a group together while one of the guys interpreted to them what was being said. There would always be a low voice in Spanish accompanying the English in our meetings.

We went over 6:30 by about five minutes, and after the meeting, the supervisor noted that we needed to finish before 6:30. From our point of view, it made perfect sense for us to have a conversation among ourselves every morning before starting time.

There was a very positive side to working with the parking meters, because it allowed you to get a flavor for all of New York City. I was driving on a daily basis in Brooklyn. Brooklyn is a wonderful place in terms of all the different people who live there. I enjoyed collecting down Nostrand Avenue, which is heavily populated by people of African descent, people from Granada, Haiti, Jamaica and many of the Caribbean islands. I enjoyed passing by the bakeries and sometimes being able to stop in and grab a quick taste of something warm-- particularly bread pudding. On any day, I might be in a heavily Caribbean section, an Italian or Jewish area, or a Latino area. There were the Latino spots over in the Bushwick section, up on Myrtle Avenue, where the beans and rice were absolutely great, with tostones dipped in garlic. There were fish patties and peas and rice on Nostrand Avenue and on Bedford Avenue; there was roti on Fulton in Bed-Stuy.

We were seeing the positive side of the people and cultures mostly through food. What an excellent way to bring diverse people together. There should be a law that everyone must experience these differences to be an educated human being. It should be taught in school. It was another way to overcome the barriers between us. And always, there was pizza; if you want a pizza, all you have to do is ask a parking meter collector, because we were the pizza experts. It was quick and fast, and that's just the way we have to move out here on a daily basis collecting the money out of these meters: quick and fast.

Sometimes when we went into a white area, we were treated differently. Our raggedy clothes, of course, magnified the problem, and when we went into a store to purchase something to eat or to look at something, we often experienced some type of racism. All sorts of assumptions were being made about who we are. People will start to hold their children's hand, and they will start to keep a watchful eye on us, being very suspicious about our movements in their neighborhood stores and businesses.

Wop-wop-wssh-waam was the constant sound, like music to my ears by now, followed by the jingle of the keys and chain. That rhythmic beat as the collector moved through a cluster of meters. So graphic were the arms, legs and hands that reach out to meters that stretch as far as the eye can see. And yet the damage occurring to our bodies as we move swiftly through these streets, in the rush for a sense of safety, was not obvious to the eye as people jump back and away from such speed. *Wop- wop-wssh-waam.*

* * *

Cosmopolitan and the International Longshoreman's Association local 1964 reached an agreement on a contract for us. We were not involved, though Jose and I did make one cameo appearance. The union attorney, Sol Bogon, looked up and said; "Welcome guys, come on in we are just wrapping up this important part. Wait until I tell you about this. You will be quite pleased." We should have this whole thing complete in perhaps another meeting. It was very weird; Mr. Masseo and these guys seem to have a lot of familiarity and things in common. These questionable dynamics are pushing all kinds of buttons in our thinking. Everybody in the room was casually going to the supermarket, except us. In fact we were the mules parked outside.

After the meeting, we left never quite understanding what was being discussed; Jose and I faked it. We were not about to sit in a room full of white folks and not at least act intelligent. We were never given any documents to read and agree on, never any briefing or pre-meeting to discuss the plan.

So Cosmopolitan and our union leadership agreed to give the drivers $10 per hour and the collectors that were there at the time Masseo signed the agreement will get $10 per hour, and everyone else would be paid $7.50. Everyone would be treated as new hires regardless of the years on the job. A grievance procedure was established. Also, seniority was established in regards to vacation and layoffs, etc. Jose had super seniority, meaning he can only be laid off after everyone else. All the rest of our issues and concerns around security, health and safety were unaddressed. There were no pension or health benefits.

Even though what we heard about the agreement did represent some important improvements in pay, reaction was mixed: Half of the guys got their wages doubled, and we did establish seniority. But other issues were not addressed, and we were not part of the process. But fortunately for all of us now, the relationship that we have with each other as workers was more important than the agreement we have with the employer. We would need it because now a tiered system existed of $10 dollars an hour for drivers and $7.50 for half the collectors. We would learn later that if you were a collector and not regular, Cosmopolitan could pay you whatever they wanted, and many non-permanent workers were earning $5 an hour. This was not what Mr. Masseo had put in writing and notarized only a few months prior.

Most of the drivers were okay with the increase, but some of the collectors were not. The evolving relationship we as workers had with each other was clearly a critical issue for Cosmopolitan, which was working against any incentives for better relationships among the workers and which continued to drive wedges among the men. Most of the newer collectors sensed that they were not in a position to speak up. From our viewpoint, the arrangement would affect productivity. Masseo had successfully found the dividing point among us, an important objective for the company. Masseo continued to bring on extra, new collectors, creating a competition for jobs and keeping things chaotic. We knew it could not last. Indeed, Mr. Masseo announced that vans would be reduced from 20 to 11, and within a few weeks, half the collectors were gone and permanent workers have been cut to 34. Another dozen came to work every day to fill in if there was absence.

Meanwhile, Jose and I were responsible in our official capacities for keeping some semblance of unity among ourselves. It was difficult. The workload grew more difficult—there were 34 regulars collecting all the parking meters in all five boroughs.

We knew that we had to win adherence to the initial Masseo agreement to pay everyone $10 an hour, and that our health and safety issues must be addressed. We maintained our daily worker meetings--they were important to balance the disarray in the field--but it was hard to balance pride in our work and dignity in our jobs with the continuing conditions.

Fortunately our spirits were far from broken, and we understood that our fight must be based on a keen awareness of our shared value to the city. These discussions were numerous, and Cosmopolitan noticed some improvement in productivity and the quality of work. Supervisor Chapman acknowledged that our meetings were proving positive, and asked only that we get into the field by 7 a.m. We took a collection and bought a coffee pot. Eli volunteered to pick up donuts every day. This added a greater sense of organization to us to maintain coffee and donuts, creating another sense of cooperation.

It wasn't long after the union contract agreement was wrapped up that Mr. Masseo disappeared. Mr. Masseo ran out of energy with whatever his mission had been. He couldn't handle the questions and the conversation that we brought to him, particularly when we would abruptly end our meeting and go find him for questions and answers; he appeared to be trying to avoid us. Jose really felt empowered by his shop steward role. We were no longer worried about being fired. We attributed Mr. Masseo's departure in part to the signing of the $10/hour agreement and notarizing it himself. We think he had no intentions of ever paying anyone $10 per hour.

His replacement was Shelley Fox, and before long, he would prove every bit of his namesake. A memo explained that Fox wanted to improve the operation and working conditions, that his style was to be upfront, that he wanted to be fair, and that his door was open. He promised to try to gain our respect and that any changes he wanted would be explained to our representatives. He went on to clarify how he wants the operation to run in terms of the collection of the meters and drew up comprehensive rules of conduct for us to follow. Mr. Fox went on to say that all of these things are part of the process of recognizing the union and finalizing the contract. We on the other hand, were not invested in Mr. Fox's rules. It might have been different if someone had sat with us to review the rules, explain the necessity of them, with some willingness to hear what we think.

By now whatever the work rules stated were insignificant to most of us and very few if any, even bother to read or pay attention to such a memo. No union contract or summary was ever distributed, and we had to learn by word of mouth what we were entitled to receive. What governed our behavior on a daily basis was our instinct or collective judgment of right and wrong, not a document.

We put up a bulletin board in the loading dock area and agreed on some worker principles: "We are workers, human beings, organized in union on our job to ensure that our labor is recognized as valuable. We see our jobs as an essential part of our lives. It is what makes a lot of other important things possible. We are organized to guarantee our right to decent work with dignity and respect." This was placed on our bulletin board in big, bold letters so that we all can see it each day as we entered the loading dock area. This was another good move that reinforced a positive message of who we were. We were no longer hiding and tucked away on the roof or off in the shadows of the dock area. We were meeting openly every morning as employees inside the Department of Transportation. The things that served to unify us were good and the things that served to divide us were bad.

It didn't matter as much what the boss says, or what the union leadership or contract said, what mattered most was what we agreed to do with each other. We were discovering our value to each other.

We planned a party to celebrate what we have accomplished so far at the Senior Citizen Center in Queens on Fresh Pond Road. A few of the guys actually cooked and a lot of the wives, moms and grandmothers prepared dishes, and we have a very well attended packed house. Mr. Fox showed up, as well as Pablo and Richie from the union. It was great to see all the extended families together, a scene at once warm and humbling. Despite a few stumbling remarks from employees who had too much to drink, it was a good occasion to note.

I made a very brief presentation, mostly about how important it was for our families to continue to be supportive, about the dangers we faced every day, about how the company was unfair and only interested in profit without concern, appreciation or compassion towards us as workers. Mr. Fox had a blank look on his face. Our families then clapped and we partied late into the night.

We felt overwhelmed with challenges with very little experience with how to handle it. There were problems with each other and problems with the boss. Jose and I were helping to organize the meetings. We would talk on the phone often during the evening. There was significant turnover among the inexperienced collectors, mostly resulting from on-the-job injuries.

It got to the point that to be a new person and not have some real get-up-and-go about yourself was something that really disturbed the guys, because people really wanted to get out in the field and finish, and not be caught with the sun coming down, stuck out there in the dark. I hated being out when the sun went down. A new collector had to really come up to speed very rapidly or they caught hell. They were teased and aggravated until they would eventually leave. There was absolutely no room for slow, lazy collectors. It was a security risk.

Because of the intensity of the job, it had been a longstanding custom that the collectors would grab something to eat before starting the daily marathon. We started a practice of all going to the same restaurant.

One morning we entered our usual breakfast spot, but for some reason, the restaurant folks were extremely abrasive with the guys. I assumed they were tired of us coming in each morning and dominating the scene, all the guys at once. I don't think the restaurant thought much about the business we brought them. The restaurant people started reacting impatiently to our food requests, and somewhat throwing our food on the table or counter and making snobbish remarks. I had some words with the owner, who essentially said we could go somewhere else if we were unhappy with the service. So the following morning, we put this item on our meeting agenda. The guys decided that we will not eat or get our food there anymore and someone suggested another spot a block away.

So after the meeting, we went to our new spot en masse. We posted a number of guys as usual to watch our vehicles. When we went inside, they were glad and opened a special room for us. They waited on us hand and foot, and we were pleased. Meanwhile the original restaurant looked fairly empty, with very few customers. They attempted to talk with some of the guys later to have us return. But it was done. Many of us were influenced by this small example of what we could do working in concert with one another.

Meanwhile, Mr. Fox was busy attempting to undermine all efforts that were separate from his control. He outlawed personal use of the vans, yet he let a few borrow vans on the weekends with his authorization. Once again we were challenged to not let these efforts divide us. Mr. Fox would call individuals into his office and attempt to socialize and hang out. He would pick the more respected guys and break out potato chips, sodas or beer, and talk sports. He started making tickets available to some and their families to go to sports events.

Eddie, whom Mr. Masseo had said would be chief of operations, used the daily meetings to bring this up. Eddie had never heard any more about his alleged promotion. Eddie said he was concerned about all the favors that Mr. Fox was giving out. He said we needed to be careful because he felt that we were being manipulated. We all agreed this was something that Cosmopolitan used to divide us.

One day Mr. Fox told Jose and me that the morning meetings needed to end. We told him that we would bring it up the next morning, which we did, drawing outrage. These meetings have come to symbolize some important developments among us. We were not about to let Mr. Fox stop our meetings.

We got Mr. Fox to our meeting and let him know we wanted an explanation for ending the meetings. He replied that while the meetings had served their purpose when there was major turmoil with John Masseo, that period was behind us now. He said; our main purpose was to work, and he would like us to concentrate on getting the job done and saw no reason why we needed to have these meeting on his time. He said it was time for the meetings to stop. Some of the guys started to remind him about the daily difficulties and the injuries, pulling up their shirts to show bruises. They reminded him of the dangers. One of the guys said; this is what should stop, not our meetings. I went on to tell him that his ball game tickets, use of the vans, potato chips and sodas would not pacify us. Mr. Fox replied that he was offended by what I said, that he did care about us and understood what we were trying to do and that I was distorting his real intent.

Our meeting broke up and the next morning we were all there as usual for our morning meeting. "The shop floor is now open!" So the first thirty minutes each morning from then on was definitely ours, and on Cosmopolitan's time.

There was one thing that we had yet to discuss at our meetings. It was something that has become widespread--the theft of the quarters from the parking meters. There was too much stealing going on and everyone knows it. Finally, a collector named Luyando was fired for stealing. It was reported in the newspaper that Luyando collected meters all the way to the van that was to pick him up. He put his canister and cart in the back of the van and then walked into a bank less than a hundred feet away and exchanged an undisclosed amount of quarters for dollar bills. Someone from the bank notified the city about what had occurred; Luyando was fired and criminal charges were filed. A few of the guys were reading their newspapers during our meeting. You heard many comments like: How stupid can you get!

This event stirred up controversy. For the first time, we opened up about the theft and what it means for us to be fighting for our fair share based on a hard day's work, yet stealing the money. It was expressed as being clearly hypocritical. Every one of us was involved, either through complicity or direct stealing. No one was blameless. No conclusions were reached but we had a very positive first discussion.

We could not figure out what to do about the health and safety issues that continued despite sending out dozens of letters. There were suggestions in our group that the union leadership was uncaring at best, and gangsters at worst.

Soon we heard that the AFL-CIO was having a big conference in New York with workshops we might want to attend. One was entitled, "Labor and Minorities." A few of us went in the hopes of gaining information and support. We observed several presentations on issues such as the garment workers and the need for people of color to be more connected to their communities, the role of women, conditions of work similar to South Africa that was going on in the South, and contracting out. There was also discussion about the impact of plant closures on minority communities and affirmative action problems internal to the AFL-CIO.

We saw that people spoke about their own issues, so I raised my hand to tell our story as parking meter collectors, from the wage cuts that happened when the city had contracted for the services to the current day dangers. I said that we were an example of the challenges faced by low-priced labor. I tell them we really need some advice, that our union leadership provided no help when we called, yet give the appearance of wanting to cuddle us like children, saying they will take care of our problems. I expressed that we were on our own, trying to figure out how to improve our working conditions and make things better for ourselves. I asked for ideas that might point us in the right direction. I took my seat. The next speaker redirected the conversation to the point he had raised his hand for previously, and spoke on another subject. The discussion went in a different direction.

This was a reoccurring dynamic in the meeting, speaker after speaker. We spoke about what we were doing, with little regard for having a dialogue, where perhaps some decisions can be made to do something together.

Afterwards, those of us who had gone tried to decipher what we had seen. It was apparent that people came to the workshop with the common interest to share information about minority issues, but were not the most helpful to one another. It was all quite foreign; we had never gone to such a meeting. When we left, the sun was out and people were crowded into Washington Square Park across the street. Everything seemed enormous; every activity has dimensions and depth, and without focus one's mind drifts endlessly. With focus, one missed something, as my eyes adjust and struggle for balance, everyone seemed so separate, distinct and yet indistinguishable.

We had no idea how other union organizations operated. This AFL-CIO meeting was our first indication of where other folks in the labor movement may be. We badly needed to feel like we belonged to something. We were eager to be embraced and comforted to stand up on the job against a rich, powerful company.

We heard that local elections were coming up and thought that maybe we could get some help if we helped someone win an election. So the guys threw out some names of elected officials they have heard about. We collected a list and decided that we would select some campaigns to get involved in.

At our meetings, generally if there was controversy around a decision, we would vote. It was understood that we would all go along with the will of the majority and respect the majority rule. Thus far, this seemed to work. Learning to communicate effectively among ourselves was like growing more arms and legs. We wanted to make outcomes better for us regarding our work, and it seemed reasonable to consider all ideas and be directed by the dominant ones. Often we saw one of the guys or another moving about during the week, trying to get support for an idea. We learned early on, that if there was no ownership on a critical decision, the likelihood of confusion was great. The responsibility of ownership around our decisions was what bound us and showed us how to work together more effectively.

We decided to work on two political campaigns--David Dinkins for Manhattan Borough President and Jitu Weusi for the Brooklyn City Council. Actually, we knew little about the candidates and their issues, except that we have heard they were interested in the concerns of poor people. We went to meet with Achuda Barkr, Jitu's campaign manager, in a large room in Bedford Stuyvesant, but had to wait; a number of us started drinking beer. Before long, there were people hanging out the windows and going outside finding alternative ways to go to the bathroom, since the space had no restroom. We really got beside ourselves; finally about half the people decided to leave. By the time Achuda returned, many were gone or quite loaded. So we decided to pick another day to meet Jitu. We took some literature and began to distribute it on our routes each day. Nevertheless, we helped drive voters for both campaigns to the polls. Dinkins won, Jitu did not.

It was noted that a few of the guys drifted in late and left early during these activities, while others really dedicated themselves to getting the task done. It was clear that this practice would have a demoralizing influence on our work and add difficulty in producing the results we were after. We discussed how the greatest of plans can work only if we were on time and paying attention to the quality of what we were doing. We talked about how always being late could be deadly to what we were trying to achieve. Everyone committed to paying close attention to the problem.

The days, weeks and months moved rapidly. We learned that Cosmopolitan management was pleased with our productivity. They knew our morning meetings had motivated and inspired the guys. Many of us were trying to adhere to our principles on the bulletin board and see our labor as valuable. It was also a dynamic that Cosmopolitan management did not control.

Before we knew it, we were in the summer heat. Collecting in the summer was better. We kept our windows down. By now we have gotten Mr. Fox to give us improved uniforms--short sleeve blue shirts for the summer and relatively new with no red stripe across it, and decently fitting pants. However this would only last a short time. They were not being maintained properly, and with all the oil and filth from the meters, they needed to be laundered regularly by the company so that we city servants could be more presentable to the public.

I finally knew where all the parking meters were in Brooklyn. I became an expert on the routes and collecting the meters. No one but us knows where all the meters were. This was one of the factors of our strength, which was the knowledge and insight of our work.

Quite often, the collecting keys were out of order. That meant the next key would not fit the appropriate meter, so we would have to know which way to handle the keys and when to flip back to the original order of keys to continue on. This could take minutes each time for a new collector and over a day could add up to hours if you were not experienced. There also were blocks or whole rows of meters for which we had no keys. This means someone else was collecting those meters. But there was no one else and if a parking meter was not collected, it would fill and then cease to operate. However, these meters operated just fine. We assumed official stealing was taking place.

One day was particularly long and slow, with inexperienced collectors. When I returned to the loading dock, everything was in an uproar. A van and the driver had disappeared on one of the routes in the Bronx. Everyone was worried about the driver, Juan Cruz, as the news spread quickly. We feared the worst has happened: One of the vans had been attacked and robbed.

The collectors never saw anything suspicious, they were in the last collection area for the day, and when it was time for them to exchange their cables and their canisters, Juan never came to pick them up. The collectors finally called the base, realizing something had happened. We were on pins and nettles waiting for news. Finally, just before nightfall, Juan was found in New Jersey tied up in the back of the van; he had been injured. He had been driving the collection route, when out of nowhere, he was attacked at gunpoint by masked robbers who snatched him and the vehicle. Juan was taken across the river, all the revenue was taken, and Juan was knocked in the head, blindfolded and left tied. A passerby heard him, notified the police and Cosmopolitan. He was taken to the hospital and released. We were all greatly relieved that he was okay. This incident sent shock waves throughout our workforce.

A few of us made a mad dash to his home to meet him there. He was very shaken and when we saw his bandaged head, the moment was emotional for all of us. The police conducted an initial interview, and there was to be a follow-up with the police and Cosmopolitan in the morning. The next morning we learned that the initial questions probed whether Juan stole the money before accepting his story.

We discussed possibly doing a press conference, recognizing that this type of robbery could happen to any of us. It was the most profound evidence of our claims, and we planned to use it to explain the urgency of doing something about our situation before one of us could be seriously injured or killed. In a few days Juan was back on his regular route.

We were starting to hear about this new drug called Crack that was out on the street and from reports given to us; it has people acting pretty crazy and will make our jobs much more dangerous. We agreed that we could not allow alcohol and drugs to be a way for us to deal with the hardships and difficulties of the job, and particularly after the fresh experience of being robbed; we need to take better precautions. We agree that alcohol and drugs will not be used on the job. We also agreed that we should try to help those among us who have problems with drugs or alcohol and that we want to have an atmosphere of support for those of us who were wrestling with these problems.

Chapter 4

Who Are We to Transform?

We initially found ourselves all somehow thrown into this same warm pot of confusion, a total reflection of our communities, always exposing the evidence, and the necessity for us to work together to make some sense of our environment. Yet we found ourselves more often than not, standing alone, separate and apart.

This was my first real job. For my last line of work, I had been a bike messenger in Manhattan, moving through the city streets, lightning fast, in top health, on my way to deliver a package. I would pull up to a parking meter, snapping my front wheel off and securing it to my back wheel, while quickly whipping out my dependable lock, and securing my bike to the meter, and then stepping fast to complete the delivery. A bus had actually hit me earlier, sending me airborne. As I glided in the air all I could think about was bracing myself for the landing. I miraculously landed on both wheels rolling and balanced. I was so thankful and yet angry with the bus driver that was in the wrong, as I pressed on to my next delivery.

I figured it was time to get away from there while I was still in one piece. Besides I needed a secure paying job with benefits.

So I came across an ad in the newspaper that read: "Time's Running Out! We're hiring parking meter collectors and drivers, and we want to fill the need immediately. If you're in good physical condition and can pass a strict background investigation, you'll enjoy all the benefits of these great jobs." It was just another lead to follow. Already I had gone to countless interviews that went nowhere.

For my initial interview I reported downtown to Cosmopolitan Care Corporation during the specified time. The place was packed with people flowing out into the hall where there were people filling out applications. What can I do I thought, hoping it would be me that got the job over these other people.

At my messenger job, we always competed with each other for the better trips, where the extra money was. I was reminded by this familiar "get a leg up on the other" drive inside of me, as I was observing and considering what moves I can make in competition with the other, looking out only for myself, before we even get to the time clock.

Everyone had to take a test for grammar and math. I passed both test and was told to report back the next day for the oral part of the interview. When I returned the next day, John Masseo, who identified himself as the VP of Cosmopolitan, interviewed me. He asked why I felt this would be a good job for me. I explained to him about my work as a bike messenger, it being dangerous and that I was looking for a better, more secure job with benefits. At this point he stopped me short and said that they did not provide benefits, but that if I was willing to work hard the money would be good. He started rambling on about a bonus system on top of the $5 an hour wage. I didn't understand the terms of the bonus system, however I nodded my head and pretended as though it was perfectly clear. I didn't want him to think that I was slow to understand. I told him that if the pay was good, I had no problems working with no benefits. He told me that I would be starting work Nov. 31st. He also told me that getting the job would depend on the results of a polygraph test that I would need to take the next day.

I found the prospect of the polygraph test frightening, I was 33 years old, formerly incarcerated, out of prison seven years ago, no arrest since. But previously I had spent a big portion of my life in and out of jail for mostly car thefts in the community and an array of assaults, graduating from junior high school and high school in jail. When I was 15 years old, during the turbulent 1960s, I started thinking very differently about the world and myself, because of the civil rights movement. However, I was still getting into trouble with the law, but finally I turned a major corner, being careful and not having any arrest in so long.

I got out of jail, got married, had two children from two previous relationships, and stayed actively involved in numerous civic activities, seeing it as a fresh start in New York. But because of my jail background, it was extremely difficult to find work and to figure out what I want to do with my life. I saw this parking meter job as a big opportunity.

The moment arrived for a polygraph test and this guy attached these wires to me and began asking me questions, I took a deep breath and just thought about Mississippi as a child, before answering each question. I had been born and raised in Los Angeles, California. I had never met my father and was raised mostly by my mom and grandmother who both worked as housekeepers.

My grandmother would often take me to Mississippi during the summer. I experienced first hand, the Jim Crow laws of segregation and discrimination that existed at that time. I began early to understand that because of the color of my skin I was to be treated differently and seen by the legal institutions in the South as inferior to whites. In fact there was a period when I agreed that we as black folks were inferior. I actually did not know enough about my history to explain any other reason why we were treated this way and why it was so widely accepted. I understood that harm could happen to me for no reason and nothing would be done about it. I saw black folks constantly pay respect to white folks, saying yes and no sir, bowing their heads and acting in an overly reverent way, using colored only facilities. I was around white folks that believed and lived out the reality of a superior role that was supported by all the legal institutions. I was afraid that I might be singled out and hurt, if not killed like Emmett Till. This was also ingrained inside of me by my relatives. White folks might ask where I was from or what was my last name? My fear would be obvious. But then over a few years the fear gradually transformed to anger. I found the black/white relationship to be despicable and intolerable.

Suddenly I was asked: Have you ever been arrested or convicted of a felony? I simultaneously reflected deeply on my Mississippi experience, repeated Mississippi quickly over and over in my head and answered, "No." My reflection on Mississippi saved the day. I passed the polygraph test, and I got the job.

I was to meet other collectors whose lives and stories touched me, affected our efforts to work as a group, and ended up influencing me in personal ways.

One day on the job, Willie, who was a collector, came to me while we were out collecting the meters and said very clearly that he did not really believe this bunch of guys could stick together, that trying to do so would be a hopeless task. He appreciated the occasional enthusiasm, but he did not think it was possible for us to be able to do anything together. He cited incident after incident of very important examples of disrespect that we showed towards each other; like the stealing of each other's stuff and the meters, the amount of near fights, the crazy "I don't give a damn" attitudes.

This conversation went on for the entire day as we jumped in and out of the van. I pleaded with him that we could not give up on each other. Willie developed some respect for me, and so I informed him that my background was just like the people he was referring to. Finally I was able to persuade him to deeply consider that we could change and do better.

I realized that many of us look at things, and see them as they are, and imagine them always being the same, never changing. I had no explanation beyond education for why we view things in this way, particularly in light of the vast number of changes that take place in our lives. Just in the last 95 years, women could vote, I no longer have to ride in the back of the bus and use separate facilities from white folks, we have the eight-hour day work laws, Social Security, unemployment insurance, environmental protections and other things. These are all changes that improved our quality of life, where for thousands of years, faced with the challenges and limitations of that period, humans were not prepared to make some of these changes. I figured it has been a kind of social evolution and should give us a reason for optimism in terms of social progress.

I knew that Willie was married, extremely religious, and always blessing the food before he ate his pizza; he was very kind, soft spoken, and one of the thoughtful guys. He would often jot down his ideas and thoughts about what we should be doing. He was constantly thinking about ways and people to contact to help us. I really appreciated this about Willie. He was a tremendous asset to the guys.

Willie, Baby Huey and Fonseca all attended the same church. Baby Huey lived up to every bit of his name. He was big and playful. He would come down and be grabbing you and going off and telling jokes and playing with everyone and saying some of the weirdest things. He would never check himself before he spoke. He said whatever came to mind. It was only his size that saved him from regularly getting his ass kicked. The things that came from his mouth were unbelievable, and so he was almost always in trouble with the guys, yet humored everyone. Perhaps the church had not gotten through to him. But under pressure as far as taking action on the job he was moving in the right direction.

Unfortunately it was the talk of the job that Baby Huey was in a relationship with Willie's wife and even worse, Willie did not know about it. I found this dynamic very painful. I had to fight back the tears, a few times while having a great planning conversation with Willie. This was just another thing affecting us really having the kind of cooperation among ourselves to get an employer to treat us in a decent way. I had the utmost respect for Willie, did not want to see him hurt, and I realized that I was quite disappointed in Baby Huey.

A number of us started to hang out after work to discuss our common issues on the job, over drinks, food, at a park or someone's house. Generally we would all climb in a car or van or we would go inside some establishment. Our talks were quite lively.

The first time I went to one of my co-worker's homes, I was really surprised. I was at Eliseo's house. He was a young collector, small in stature, about 20 years old, quiet yet never backing down from a conflict, always coming across in an aggressive way, asking those escalating the issue questions, with a wonderful wife and baby, living not far from the job. I quickly learned that another collector was visiting Eliseo's home, by the name of Lockjaw. Eliseo and Lockjaw were close friends. Lockjaw was in another room counting quarters, not startled by my presence in the house. Eliseo had invited me over, and now he was asking me to be cool about seeing a co-working with stolen coins. Eliseo said the practice was widespread, which I knew already. They acted as if I should be a part of their scene, always inviting me out.

Lockjaw got his name from being a little stocky and having a protruding jaw like the cartoon character. He loaded my car down with different women on a few occasions, always full of hanging out ideas. He had ambitions of joining the police force. This job was just to carry him over until the police force calls him from the waiting list. He would say he had already passed the test and was on a list to be called to start at the academy for the New York City Police Department. Lockjaw would often talk about how he could not wait to get on the force. There was money to be made, games to be played and he knew how to play every single one of them, he said. So I kept the whole stealing incident to myself as usual.

Most of my co-workers would never bring such foolishness into their home. I went by Eddie Montalvo's house. Eddie was a collector, and his family very nice. He had three small children, more than anyone else on the job and I came to love them dearly. Eddie always carried himself like an old man. He was of Puerto Rican descent and very fair complexioned. He has a very nice wife. When I came over, she cooked. She didn't work, stayed home and took good care of the three children. It was through her effort with the meals and cleanliness of the house that you get a feeling of stability that somehow almost overshadows the obvious poverty, a skill that many poor families have mastered. Eddie took his life and family very serious. I liked Eddie and his family a lot, and would find myself there often to talk with him and play with his children, who were quite fond of me.

Jaime, a veteran collector, was the longest on the job. His hands were very bruised and calloused, and he was very short and small in stature. It was difficult to say how old Jaime was. He had a problem, looking yellow and having some type of hepatitis. Desperate for cash he sold his tools to one of the guys. He would be too loaded for anyone to steal quarters with him. But he got the job done each day, and never slowed us up. I met his family and son over at his house one evening, hanging outside with Jaime. His son, then 8 or 9 years old, said he wanted to be a lawyer. I remember looking up and down the street, at all the scarcity, thinking it to be remarkable to hear this young child articulate such a thing. You could tell he was trying to pull things in a different direction than Jaime; he seemed to be such a reverent young person. Jaime on the other hand, would often approach women, while we were loading or unloading ourselves to collect the meters, and say; excuse me mam, do you have the time? And while she is about to give him the time, he'd say, "I got the place." Laughter would ring out from the guys, as the woman's face showed signs of having been insulted, she moved on. A few of the younger guys would even attempt to imitate Jaime. JD and Jaime were close, both started with the same contractor.

JD, a collector, had cleaned up his alcoholism, and was a very clean-cut, respectful black man, but had relapses from time to time; he would disappear from work and would be on and off the job. JD was a very quiet person and he lived with one of his parents in Long Island. He was highly knowledgeable about a lot of social things. He shared a copy of the operational manual of the previous contractor. He seemed to be very serious about his recovery. It was as if he could not really get close to anyone, and he had to be totally wrapped up in his personal bout. And though alcohol was the problem he was fighting, it was also as if a part of his recovery plan, that dealing with other people was a problem he had to be careful of as well.

The six Bronx Boys were an interesting group; they always rode in together. Andino and Hector mainly drove the others, while continuing their constant discussion over job problems we were having and specifically what should be done. They took a specific pride in being from the Bronx, and it was like this meant they were supposed to be acting wild all the time, which they made every effort to demonstrate. I would go to the Bronx to visit them occasionally, and they would quickly locate each other, bringing out their pit bulls, and all their bling bling -- jewelry, caps and sneakers. They seemed to get along with each other just fine. It was just understood that they would be talking trash to each other, with an occasional blow to the chest, filled with laughter and symbols of affectionate, yet degrading love. For the most part we would hang out eat and drink on the street. The good thing about them was that they could get serious, and we had good conversations. Robles and Jay would make a conscious effort to pull together agreement among the guys.

One of the Bronx boys was Foreman, who was from Jamaica. He spoke Spanish, which he had learned through the ties and friendships in the Bronx. I admired what he had accomplished in learning another language. I thought of him as being quite sharp even though he did not promote himself in this way. Foreman was very short and was somewhat small initially, but then he started working out and overnight became solid and built with muscles. This was an amazing achievement.

There was Gonzales who was short and frail, but very fiery, like a little Chihuahua dog, loud and outspoken for his size. Gonzales was very slick in his mannerisms. I will never forget him and Forman hovering over a heater that didn't work in the van, refusing to go out and collect the meters because it was dark, cold and their hands hurt. What a sight, and they had been competing to get the smallest amount of keys, trying to manipulate each other as well as me. It was quite a situation, but we astonishingly somehow finished that day.

Jose Aponte, a driver, was always speaking up and wrestling with the difficulty of us sticking together. Jose had two children, two girls, and a wife. He was very solid, principled, serious and determined. He was very much a family man. He was on a local baseball team, played basketball, bowled and lifted weights. Both of Jose's parents were born in Puerto Rico. His parents did factory work, saved their money and came to NY at the age of 18, and gave birth to 4 boys, two of whom were twins, of which Jose was one. His father went to work performing various cleaning jobs and eventually ended up with a maintenance job at Brooklyn College until he was able to open a neighborhood grocery store. Jose's mother mostly remained home to raise the four boys. Jose finished high school and got married to his high school sweetheart at sixteen years old. By the age of 20, he and his wife had two children. He had worked odd jobs before the parking meters. Two of Jose's three brothers worked with us as collectors as well -- his twin, Angelo, and younger brother, Felix. As with most of us, the parking meter job was their first real job.

The three Aponte brothers were very much alike in size and height and also in principles. They were always very respectful to others, believed in the good of others, and did not take abuse. However in terms of personalities, they were very different. Angelo, who had started with the previous contractor, was a driver who was very quiet and laid back. He spoke very slowly. He had a daughter and was married. We often called him *la muerte*, meaning "the death," because he walked and talked so slowly; we'd get a big laugh out of this, while he always kept a serious composure. Of the three, Angelo was the most cautious and least easy going. Felix, on the other hand, was more recent to the meters – he was a collector who was barely 21 and a part of the really young set among the guys. While Felix loved the bling, bling, he was quite mature and thoughtful. He had a baby with his girlfriend, though the relationship was rocky. Felix was a hard working collector, perhaps the second fastest, always outspoken on the point of us working together. I looked to Felix and his two brothers for direction; together they were a part of the glue that helps to hold us together. Their mom was a magnificent person who regularly went to play Bingo—and won. She would not hesitate to cook for us, introducing me to Puerto Rican food. Jose's wife Betsy taught me my first salsa step in dance. They lived in a two-story row house with a basement in east Brooklyn. Their entire family, wives, children and all shared this wonderful caring home of beautiful people.

There was very little turnover among the drivers. In fact, the first driver to leave was replaced by Luis Cruz, who was hired because he had had a great deal of experience with the previous contractors. In fact, Armored Express, the previous contractor, had enticed Luis and others not to continue to work with the meters under Cosmopolitan. They were told that they would be paid more money if they remained with Armored Express, to do deliveries in the city. As it turned out, this proved to be an effort by Armored Express to prevent Cosmopolitan from having a successful transition. Armored Express failed to live up to its part of the bargain of more money and so Luis and a few other guys also returned to the parking meters looking for work. Luis, too, was married. He was from the Dominican Republic where his parents did factory work before his father worked in a furniture store. Luis was the oldest of four children who moved to New York in 1965 and eventually relocated to New Jersey.

Luis played basketball in high school. He received a scholarship to play ball at Pace University. Later he played professional ball in the Dominican Republic, where he met his wife. After returning to New Jersey, Luis was looking for work and heard about the parking meters from a ball-playing friend and ended up a parking meter collector.

Luis had a lot of ambition, constantly planning to do things with his life and with his wife, always talking about improving himself and doing better and buying a home. He didn't plan to be a parking meter collector forever. It was a pleasure meeting such an enthusiastic person. Luis really knew all the areas quite well. He also goes back a ways with some of the guys and I could talk to him about problems and ideas. We would talk about what we can do to improve the quality of these jobs and make them meet our goals in life. He was impressive in these discussions and begins immediately to play a very positive role in our morning meetings.

One of the guys noticed that Max had not been attending the meetings for a couple of weeks. In fact, he had been loading up his van very early and was failing to attend the pre-work meetings. Also, the boss had been letting him take the van home every evening, Max decided he would try to improve the appearance of the van with car polish, the result being a very polished up wreck.

After one of our meetings, I went over to Max and asked him to attend, that we considered them mandatory. He shrugged, and did not attend again the next day. A few of the other guys spoke to him about this as well. He told them that he would come, but he really wanted to hurry up and finish each day because he had other things to do with his life. Finally, Luis Cruz and I approached him. I did the talking. I told him we found it insulting that he could not find the time to be at the meetings, because this was where decisions were made and where our priorities were established. I told him there was still a lot to be done to improve our conditions and we needed his support. It started to get aggressive before Luis intervened. Later, Max said he would like to talk with me. We had a beer, and a decent discussion about his life, my life and how we needed to really work together to improve our lives. After that, Max was at every meeting from that point on and it wasn't long before he was speaking up and taking the lead around critical issues.

Max was born in 1964. His parents couldn't raise him at that time, and they get help from his grandparents on his father's side, which eventually became who he calls mother and father and who raised him. His biological mother did domestic work in Puerto Rico. His father worked on a sugar cane plantation. In the late 1950s, his parents came to New York. Raphael "Max" Medina was born in Brooklyn and lived across the street from the Brooklyn shipyards, living with his grandparents, who both came to New York around the same time. His grandmother worked in a garment factory until her asthma forced her to stop work; his grandfather was a bookie and later became a janitor at the movie theater. Max started work at the racetrack when he was nine years old, walking horses on the weekend. He would work at the racetrack until he started with the parking meters in 1982 at age 18. He had dropped out of school when he was 16 to work full time at the racetrack; he had a child when he was 17. Max had worked with CDC and Armored Express and was quite disturbed with how his wages had dropped.

Max and I sometimes purchased some blackberry brandy and poured it over ice cream and ate it on the job. It would make for a very exciting day. We could almost forget the danger, the fear, the nervousness, aggravation and pain from our various injuries. In the colder months, the alcohol would certainly keep us warm. And it helped push the issue of alcohol and drug use to the agenda of our morning meetings.

Until we addressed it, we would drink on the job. I had done so on occasion, particularly to keep warm. Luis Ortiz was someone with whom I might share some rum. Luis worked even faster when he was drinking. We would argue and curse each other the whole day. Luis Ortiz had some kind of substance abuse background, always appearing to be ready to go off the curve.

Ortiz was having a big problem with his eyes; he said it was from stuff that got onto his hands from the meters. He and others complained often that there were chemicals on the meters that were causing rashes.

Ortiz was a very smart person, but odd. He was very knowledgeable of the collection areas and was very quick. But no one could ride a cart down slopes while collecting the parking meters except Ortiz. He would be throwing his hands up, like he was ready to fight, grabbing and punching folks here and there. If Ortiz perceived weakness, he would take advantage. He referred to a few of the guys as cute, and he would jokingly demand kisses, pat them on their behinds and make sexual overtures toward them. This was all done in humor, but it was constant insanity like this that Ortiz has fun with. What a character.

Ortiz had a very outspoken sense of what it means to be a man, though I suppose it was not that uncommon among poor, working class men of color in NYC. It was quite familiar to me. If he sees someone drinking a soda with a straw, he will come over and say, "What you got a straw for? Only punks drink sodas with a straw. A man doesn't do that." He would say this often, with a straight face to some of the guys, and would always be telling someone that they were not a man or that they need to be a man and take a stand.

At a party, Ortiz had both his sons with him. One was about three, the other about four or five. They both were crying and looking so serious, angry and mean. He motioned to them to take a drink of beer, talking about he was making them men. He would pull the glass over to them saying, "Here, have a drink." They would turn their noses up and look at him in disgust.

On the other side of this, there was loyalty, and honesty about Ortiz. He spoke his mind and he can be counted on. He was not one to lie and deceive others. Some think, in fact, that he was crazy. I found him quite interesting. I have been to his home and met his wife who was very nice and concerned about him, and I was sure she was an anchor and the main reason that he was able to keep his focus and bearings to the extent he does. You could tell he really respected his wife.

Eventually we recognized that alcohol and drugs were a problem among the parking meter collectors. There were always a few guys that would come in at the end of the day attempting to disguise the fact that they were drunk. Some were young hard-core alcoholics. Some people used cocaine on the job. It appears to be a recreational drug for those that did this. Alcohol, on the other hand, appears to be a greater threat for a few parking meter collectors. And as the use of crack cocaine spread, it was Ortiz, who having experienced this drug first hand, finally helped persuade us to face it.

Ortiz like most of us had the utmost respect for Eli. Their families were somehow connected, and he would never even jokingly mess around with Eli. Eli had an infectious impact on all of us, a very religious person; he always contributed random acts of kindness. Rarely did he have anything to say, but he showed by example. He volunteered to pick up different people and bring them to work. He stopped on the way in everyday to pick up donuts for our meeting. Eli was very short in statue, but in very good shape. Eli was the fastest collector and had the second longest time on the job next to Jaime. Elis's quickness has earned him the nickname "Grandmaster." Normally the drivers will say, I have these collectors going out with me, but when Eli was around the driver will say I'm going out with Eli. You were almost guaranteed to get back in early if Eli was a part of the team.

Often when I pulled in, I would find Eli with a handball beating the guys or playing alone. I understand that Eli had a lot of brothers, more than six in his family and he was the youngest. His father was much older than usual. The guys said this really contributed to a serious, determined Eli, who was also taking business classes, was married with two children. You had to really be there for a while to know what a powerful impact Eli had on the unity of the guys, he silently helped us maintain our moral bearings, always wanting to help others do the right thing, no foolishness, very honest, and definitely the hardest worker.

Another interesting person was Lang, a much older white guy. He had retired from his previous job with a pension. He was very quiet around our job concerns. He was always a mostly one-word kind of guy, a yes or no person, Lang guarded and protected whatever his thoughts were and was quiet on his route as well. He didn't appear to be very interested in anything we were doing, though he was always there and cooperative. On occasion he made it clear that his life was pretty much situated and that he would go along with whatever we thought was best, which he actually did for the most part. Lang was a straight up guy. If not before me, he was always the second person to pull his van into the dock for loading. The collectors complained however that he stayed in the van too much and never would come out to help them collect. Also it was believed that he carried a firearm to protect himself in the event of a robbery.

Also there was Fisher. We started with the meters on the same day. He was homeless prior to the parking meters. In fact he lived out of a homeless shelter when we first started with the meters. We all knew he had very little to fall back on, yet he operates as though he has everything to gain by working with the effort to make our work environment better. Fisher was a very quiet person, slim, medium height and always walks somewhat hunched over. He never spoke up at our meetings, but was always up front and no task was too great. He was kind to everyone and quite distrustful of the system, but never talked about what happen to him and family. He was one the few white guys on the job, he simply worked hard and everyone respected his dedication and support. When you think of Fisher it helps to get our bearings about what this effort was about on a personal level.

It was an important challenge to have all of us pulling in the same direction, being as diverse as we are. However I have noticed that when we could set up events to get us to a common understanding and have agreement on what the problem is, the chances of us reaching a strong agreement on what to do increased.

Chapter 5

Uncovering Mysteries Together

At one morning meeting, we agreed that in order to make effective decisions, we needed more information about parking meters, contracts and what the city's history showed about collections. Someone suggested starting at the Hall of Records.

We were also distracted by the disturbing news that Felix had been arrested for the killing of a bouncer at a nightclub. The bouncer, we were told, was throwing his weight around. Felix would go to prison, barely escaping a life sentence.

Jose and I volunteered to explore the history of the parking meters in New York City. Having no real experience at doing any investigation like this, we awkwardly went into the Hall of Records asking for information on parking meters. They referred us to the Municipal building and the New York Public Library on 42nd street. An attendant at the Municipal building shared a collection of articles, local laws and charters about parking meters.

The first thing we read was "First Parking Meters Used in City Tomorrow," dated Sept. 14, 1951 about an installation of 270 meters on 125th Street in Harlem, a project aimed at promoting greater turnover of available curb space and expediting traffic flow by eliminating double parking. Workers were painting lines and sinking stanchions on both sides of 125th Street between Lenox and 7th Avenue; a dime would allow one hour's parking. By the end of October, according to the article, the city would have meters on the Lower East Side, the Borough Hall section of Brooklyn, the Fordham section of the Bronx and Sunnyside Queens, expandable to the whole city. The 1,427 meters would cost about $75,000, but were projected to earn $220,000 per year.

I was astonished that this important experiment was first taking place in the black/Latin, working-class community and though I looked for information as to why, I found no reason. Why not start such an experiment in a richer neighborhood, like on Madison Avenue or Wall Street instead?

A document entitled, "The Local Laws of the City of New York" for the year 1949 explained that the city had wanted to amend the city Charter to allow meters, but apparently it took two years to start the project.

There was more: By 1961, revenue was up to $6 million per year; in 1962, there was a lot of competition for the contract to manufacture meters. In 1964 there was a scandal and investigation in which the City Council purchased 52,000 meters in1961 and 1962 at $2.6 million without a public bidding, and there was a perjury indictment against Duncan Parking Meters, which still manufactures most of the parking meters in the US. Duncan apparently paid $25,000 to get the contract.

In 1966 city officials discovered parking meter theft rings, including raids on workshops where parking meter keys were being manufactured. A 1966 article outlined a history of thefts, prompting city purchase of tamper-proof meter locks.

City officials decided in 1973 to get more money from the existing meters by starting 30-minute red-posted meters, yellow-posted meters for 1-hour, and a blue post for 2-hour meters. By then 3,000 meters were charging 25 cents. By 1974, New York City had 67,000 parking meters. The numerous accounts of meter theft by the parking meter collectors who worked for the City continued until 1969, when officials decided to outsource the collection work.

There also was controversy around the companies that repaired the meters, whose employees we saw on our routes, unscrewing and replacing parts on installed meters. What we saw was that these employees were almost all white, with comparatively very nice vehicles, performing minimal work. Our understanding was that the current contractor, S&D Maintenance, got $15 million per year to do this repair work and that the contractor we work for was getting $1.5 million plus forty four cents a meter for collections in all five boroughs.

A 1978 article said that S&D took over the contract for two years with 15,000 broken meters for $6 million, at $4.70 per meter. By 1976 they were talking about refurbishing 1,000 more meters to handle quarters. All the extra funds will be for roads and highway improvements. An earlier maintenance corporation called Metco Maintenance had the contract for 12 years at $4 million per year.

At a library in Staten Island, we found an encyclopedia that outlined the history of parking meters, first used in this country in 1935 in Oklahoma City. In 1933, Oklahoma City was a boomtown, and there were many complaints about parking. The authorities started removing people's car tires and placing notes on cars about parking. In 1935 they developed the meter; the primary concern apparently was not revenue. Later In the first court challenge the city argued that they needed to charge a fee to pay police to enforce parking regulations. The proceeds were being used for the public's welfare.

Some 2,000 years ago in ancient Rome the authorities tried to control congestion with the parking of chariots. Apparently Julius Caesar banned the chariots from business areas of the city during certain hours of the day and this ban didn't apply to chariots on religious or state business.

We also learned that in Cuba during the 1950s, there was a big scandal around the parking meters. In Havana, members of the police ordered all the money collected from the meters and delivered to them. Police were seen dragging coins to a plane, fleeing the advancing takeover by the revolution.

Jose and I reported about what we had learned, and found our co-workers were most impressed with reports about stealing and they laughed about the Roman chariots. It seemed every four or five years, groups of workers were getting caught stealing. Their general reactions showed us that we needed more information to feel ready for challenges. Actually, we came away with more questions than answers. The age of transportation promoted by the success of the automobile industry had challenged public understanding and needs about street parking. We also learned London installed their first parking meters only in 1957. We wondered why the experience was later there, and whether the British had placed the first implementation in a working class or ethnic community too. Was the location of parking meters initially related to race or class?

The lesson for us was that curiosity and investigation produced valuable information, vital to us being able to understand our role and purpose. It made us more knowledgeable and equipped.

* * *

Jose told us there was a big union meeting coming up, and that we should all plan to attend. Some of us thought ill of the union leadership. Most of us thought that by paying dues, we should not have to do much and that the union's role was to fix everything. Since the union leadership had not proved responsive, we were disappointed and felt that the union was not doing a good job. We were not sitting back, but our understanding had not yet caught up with what we as workers needed to do to achieve success. We were praising ourselves for defending ourselves, but were still expecting that the union leadership should be the ones doing the things that we were doing.

As things stood, our union leaders said we just needed to call when we had a problem, and that they would take care of it-- which I thought increasingly was quite distant from reality, reminding me of a traveling salesman that came to my childhood home. The union leadership actually promoted the idea that we could be successful by relying on them with very little of our own activity needed. So how and why would the employer respect the employees? How would we learn cooperation and organizational skills? A few of us came to see that people from outside our workplace could help, but that we never should expect them to do everything for us or to determine for us what we want and how to get it. Because how can someone from the outside consistently get the employer to do what we cannot get the employer to do.

I realized that every time we read the paper, look or listen to the media, or sit in a classroom of a teaching institution, we were being taught that working people have no interest in working cooperatively among themselves. At the heart is a view that human beings have some natural inclination toward greed. So at all cost everyone must be careful when we get together. We get all these subtle messages of looking out for number one and staying away from the group. You should be different! Have your own individual opinion, and not someone else's. Don't be led around by some group. Be careful of the cult. Most working people do not successfully get through the barrage of notions that keep us suspicious and disconnected from each other.

Surprisingly the ones mostly suspicious of the group, as a way to do better probably were ourselves -- working people. On the other hand, big businesses have always practiced a form of working together, being a team player and carrying out the desires of the corporate board. It was an accepted way to conduct business. The question was what's a small group of workers going to do to overcome these views that keep working people divided?

* * *

On one particular morning meeting—it was Oct. 3, 1985--Jose said it really was time for us to decide on a direction. Luis said that we need to make a deeper commitment to each other, to show more trust, adding that it was really messed up that we wanted the city and Cosmopolitan to do things for us that we were not prepared to do for each other. You couldn't leave anything around without worrying that it wouldn't be there when you got back. Max also spoke about the urgent need for us to quit treating each other in negative ways. The theft has to stop. We need to be respectful to the public.

And so we all formed a big circle and held each other's hands. We took an oath that we would not take anything from one another on the job without permission; that we would respect the public on the streets while performing our jobs; that we would not steal from the parking meters, and we only want what we deserve as compensation for the hard work that we perform every day. We all vowed and made serious promises to each other to work together and not allow anything to come between us.

From this day on, things really changed. You could put something down and come back and it was still there. The time was right to heighten the sense of respect among ourselves. A few lagging in complying, but we were patient, and saw that condemnation by the group brought everyone into line.

Very quickly after these decisions, a number of guys quit drinking as much or quit using drugs. You started to see people not having the time to hang out after work. You started to hear about guys starting to associate with more religious experiences and attending church more often and being involved in other civic activities. Clearly there was change going on among us. It was as though folks found something that gave them a sense of themselves in the way they needed, so that they could take the next step to advance themselves. Jose in particular, started participating in religious services more.

Exercise was the biggest hit, it seems like everyone was doing something. Folks played basketball together, handball together, and a number of guys would join teams. I would run to and from work sometimes and sometimes ride my bike to and from work.

Other discussions focused on other public service workers such as the PG&E, the phone man and mail carriers about their dress and attitudes toward the public and how we could learn a lot from how they conduct themselves, especially toward women. In our meeting, we talked about catcalls to women as an example, saying how necessary it was to change this image of ourselves and to start to think of ourselves as being important people, with an important role.

We discussed the fact that we were bringing in millions of dollars that were being used to underwrite city services to make transportation and the highways safer. We began to understand that we needed to be proud of what we were doing to be able to carry ourselves in a proud way. This will also help produce among the public a sympathetic appeal to our plight. It proved an effective message and if someone in the field was conducting himself in a ridiculous way, it will eventually be brought up and discussed at our meeting.

Even though the public attitudes of some around us were not sympathetic, our clothes might not be as nice, and the vehicles were awful, we were in a fight for dignity. We understood that we could not continue to belittle and disrespect ourselves because in doing that we were playing right into the hands of a stereotype about ourselves, as being inferior human beings.

We would often bring out how amazing it was that the current and previous employers never told us what a valuable contribution we were making to the City of New York, bringing in 60-80 million dollars a year. As workers, we had to discover the significance of our work. No one had ever said that this labor of ours meant anything. At our meetings the guys constantly said that the disregard around the importance of our jobs by the city and Cosmopolitan was all by design, because to show or express that our work was important was to agree that we should be treated better.

Wop-wop-wssh-waam was the sound of these parking meters being collected fast. It was starting to get cold again, and the injuries were mounting anew. There were too few people for so much work. People were walking stiffly from the strenuous routine. Guys constantly discussed the pain they endured in different parts of their body from the work. Our vehicles were starting to break down more often, and complaints were up. Often we would be spending time with our loads in the back of the van, while a mechanic was fixing it.

My van was starting to stall when I pressed the gas pedal, and nothing was being done about it. This was bad because we had no security, and we could not afford any delays. I decided that I would give my van a decent burial, which was something you will hear someone say when the vehicle gets bad like this. Cane syrup was perfect for the gas tank at the end of the day. I conducted a funeral service while one of the collectors, imitated the sound of a trumpet funeral dirge.

In the morning I was issued a nice rental van for a few days that had air conditioning and FM radio, and then I received another dilapidated vehicle, and after the canisters hit the back door a few times, we were tying it shut. We also often complained about the carts because they kept breaking down. We would be out there with a disabled cart, trying to pull it down the street, loaded down with at least a hundred and twenty five pounds of coins, with one wheel wobbling or coming off.

But then there were people like Eli, the grand master, who knew how to repair his equipment quickly and could move along those streets so rapidly, collecting the meters. *Wop- wop-wssh-*

waam! Eli was moving down the street collecting the meters faster than an average person can walk. It was understood that no one could beat him when it comes to a race. But there were others whose pace was really picking up. It made the days feel safer. Everyone was learning the routes really well, so we were able to move quicker to complete the day.

The older people were teaching the newer ones about how to move through the meters quickly. The workforce was starting to stabilize in terms of turnover. People were starting to stick with it, starting to feel there was something to fight for here. We had a rhythm.

* * *

With a big union meeting approaching, Jose sought instructions. Our guys agreed that it was mandatory for all to attend – 15 carloads of us went to a community center site in New Jersey. Pablo, who seemed amazed to see all of us, greeted us. Pablo approached Jose and slipped him a note; Pablo wanted Jose to nominate the son of union president Richard Costello, as treasurer of the local.

Costello opened the meeting, announcing that there would be elections on this day, and that to vote, you had to be a member in good standing and that meant to be a dues-paying member for one year. It was November and I realized we would not qualify, as we have not been members for one year. Jose and I look at each other as if to say, "I guess we won't be voting." Jose was perplexed about how to respond to the mixed messages. I told him I did not know how to respond. Maybe it was a test or something. On the stage area with Costello was an attractive woman with a large rolodex and her fingers were moving lightning fast to confirm if the person making the nomination was a member in good standing. There were about 150-200 people in the meeting, mostly black and Latino men from various small companies, though ours was the largest single group present.

As it turned out Richard Costello Sr. was reelected the president and Richard Costello, Jr. his son, as secretary-treasurer, both the only nominees. Jose had made the nomination of the son.

As soon as we would leave, everyone was going to talk about the fact that we had only been members for nine or ten months and we had not been members for a year and so therefore we were not eligible to vote. To them, this felt corrupt and untrustworthy, our guys felt used, and this seemed an important blunder by the union officials that they never will recover from in the eyes of the parking meter collectors.

Jose felt as if he may have done the union leaders a favor that could translate into getting us more help. But all such hopes were quickly erased, as the union leadership remained a virtually nonexistent presence in our lives. However, we felt that this situation now had gained our official blessing.

The conduct of the union leadership was the topic of attack for weeks thereafter, with many questioning why we were paying dues or with this union organization at all. My only argument was that we did not want to be out here alone, without any back up, support or legal advice, to counter Cosmopolitan, and we needed to figure out how to address getting a better union replacement.

As we talked about how as workers that we were the union; we realized that there was no other practical choice for us. Our strength was based on whatever we had been able to put together among ourselves. When we began our search to join a union, we initially had thought we were going to find a union that would solve all our problems for us.

It was starting to make sense to some of us that the way we were operating was an important part of how the union should work. All we really needed from the union leadership was the formal training so that we could work with each other and the public more effectively, and the second thing would be the legal support. Unfortunately, this outfit to which we paid dues, masqueraded in our midst, only wearing the costume and mask of the union and providing no real substance.

I occasionally thought about how to play less of a role. I had tired of doing all this work, being involved in all the conversations and plans of action. I wanted to spend my time doing something else for a while. I attempted to chill out for a moment. However, I noticed that every time our pace slowed up, management appeared to escalate their efforts to do what they want. Management always wanted to meet one on one with some of us. There was always a rumor of a crackdown policy, or a new work rule. It was clearly a "them and us" situation, and we were encouraged by what we had among ourselves. There was love, care and concern for each other developing among us, and it could be felt at every meeting we attend now. This represents even more than what some of us have at home with our families.

We came to work every day to serve the people of New York City, but were not dressed properly, had no security, suffered unsafe conditions and inadequate vehicles. We went into the cold, going from meter to meter, turning each key as it crushed into our hands, and into our bones. We endured each day with the anticipation and dreams that we would succeed in creating a decent life for our families and ourselves. This feeling was all recent, and linked to our sense of respect for one another. We were no longer pulling and tearing at each other.

There should be institutions that exist to showcase positive models among working people on the job, especially since most are working people. It should be on TV and promoted by the media, a mandatory subject in all classrooms. This should be a social program that the government is responsible for. I wonder why we have to be like Christopher Columbus on this issue.

Wop-wop-wssh-waam! We were getting it on, working both sides of the street and we were lighting it up in Brooklyn. We were getting down. I was in my vehicle and totally energized over how fast the collectors were moving. We were not missing a one. It was cold outside and the parking meter collectors were getting hot, as we transform the abuse we receive into determination and drive.

We did hear from the union: The ILA local wanted us to make a contribution to some workers that have been locked out of their jobs at a factory in Newark. We agreed to do so, especially because it was close to Christmas and how terrible it was that these workers were being replaced. We took pride in the fact that no one else really knew where the parking meters were but us. So we felt that it was highly unlikely for us to be replaced in that same sort of way.

Jose, Luis Cruz, Max and I were a sub-committee that met regularly. We developed a questionnaire from our morning meeting, to ask all our co-workers. We divided up the guys among our subcommittee to improve communications. The idea was that we don't want to leave one stone unturned in terms of getting ideas from the guys and having their investment in whatever will come next. We get 100% agreement. What a great way to begin a new year.

* * *

The newest challenges were coming from outside our immediate world.

From all accounts, the use of crack had become epidemic, threatening our safety. Collectors reported that people were approaching us looking for our money, like some kind of "walking dead" after the coins in our canisters.

Bribery and corruption scandals had started to unfold in the city of New York, particularly concerning awarding of city contracts. The city contracts issue was no surprise to us because we definitely have a story to tell about how Cosmopolitan had acquired the contracts to collect New York City's parking meters.

There was scandal over charges of extortion involving an official in the city's parking violations bureau who accepted a $5,000 bribe from a company to collect overdue fines for the parking violations Bureau. The city cancelled several contracts, started to change rules, and talked of reducing outside debt collection agencies. The former director of the Parking Violations Bureau was charged with having extorted a bribe from a bill collecting company; everyday there was more information coming out that widens the scope of the investigation to eight or nine city agencies. The Koch administration was scrambling.

Donald Manes the Borough President of the Borough of Queens was also implicated in the whole issue of the Parking Violations Bureau, and then was found dead. People start to step forward and say that they have received pay offs, from the car racing, there were implications of bribery, the Queens Democratic Party records were seized by the FBI, and resignations start to pour in. In quick order, the Director of the Parking Violations Bureau resigned, followed by the Parking Violations Bureau's Counsel, the Transportation Commissioner, and the City's Commissioner of Investigations resigned.

So we were astonished about how all these events have started to come together so rapidly.

We convened a meeting among ourselves, dedicated to examining what the series of events meant for us. The guys brought up what they experienced in terms of how Cosmopolitan was awarded its city contract. Some of our co-workers had been instructed by city officials to work with Cosmopolitan before they were even awarded the contract to give Cosmopolitan information they needed to beat out others in the bidding process.

We agreed to meet with a lawyer, Vernon Mason, to share what we knew about Cosmopolitan, adding our complaints about working conditions. Mason and his colleague Fred Brewington agreed to represent us without pay because of the social justice significance of the case. We developed a fact sheet and catalogued our injuries, and set up a press conference. The lawyer pointed out the irony that people like ourselves who are important victims go unnoticed, virtually invisible as the scandal swirled.

It was at this point in time that we all got familiar with the terminology, "dilapidated vehicle," which became part of our everyday vocabulary in terms of describing the vans. Although we may have had many communications challenges, in that some may not even have spoken English very well, we would all say that our vans were "dilapidated vehicles" very clearly.

Photo from Parking Meter Collectors' file

Parking meter collectors presented their grievances at a crowded press conference with lawyer, Vernon Mason.

We deeply believed that public pressure was possible to address our issues. Cosmopolitan management remained unaware of what we were doing, which illustrated the strength of the bond that existed among us. You could see the optimism in our body language as we go to work daily, *wop-wop-wssh-waam*, and *Baya!* was the scream.

It was time for the press conference – after work, of course. More than 30 of us crowded into the law office to nervously explain our issues. We told the horror stories that we experienced daily at the hands of Cosmopolitan and the

Department of Transportation. The reporters asked numerous questions about our work; how we performed it, how many meters we collected every day, how difficult our work was and the conditions of the vehicles that we drove every day. We rolled up our shirts, took off portions of our clothing and showed them the conditions of our hands, our bodies, and our injuries. There were scars on just about everyone, some serious, with physical contortions on a few of the guys, where an area of their body did not heal properly, and since folks had no health benefits there was nothing they can do about it.

We gave numerous accounts of our life-threatening security problems and the deplorable working conditions. Juan Cruz talked about being robbed, and others explained how on numerous occasions they took steps that avoided being robbed. Max described an electrical fire in his van; Baby Huey shared details of a robbery attempt; flying canisters in a van lacking seats had injured Kenny Vargas.

Luis Cruz gave an account of having been pulled upstairs on several occasions by Department of Transportation officials and directed to meet with Cosmopolitan representatives sometime before they were awarded the contract and to explain to them how the meters work and how collections on a daily basis were conducted. No other bidder was afforded the opportunity to get inside information of this nature. We were also demanding that we be made City workers and that we start to obtain all of the rights and condition of work as other city employees.

Despite the information, there was no newspaper story the next day, while reporters continued to verify what they had heard. Still, I was interviewed on radio station WBLS, switching my Brooklyn route with another driver in Manhattan, to be available during lunch hour, and be interviewed. The live interview went well, some of us listened in. We also met with a community group called "Journey for Justice," that worked closely with our lawyer, and started attending meetings of the Coalition of Black Trade Unionists.

The Daily News story broke entitled "Collection Of Charges, In The Story They Tell" by Earl Caldwell, he described it as another piece of the scandal of New York, and they are the workers who collect the money from the parking meters all over New York City. He described in detail the discrimination and exploitation that takes place, our working conditions and how the work force had changed from White workers to people of color predominately. Then the Amsterdam News, followed by the New York Times, and then it was the Daily Challenge and Big Red, which are two Black newspapers, as well as the City Sun.

By the end of one day, Mr. Fox called Jose and me to discuss the coverage, saying that the company was being hurt, which, in turn, will hurt the workers. We just listened. By contrast, the guys were jubilant over the press coverage. Finally it feels as though we were doing something. Returning to the law office, we developed next steps, including creation of a list of community leaders and elected officials that we should contact.

Meanwhile, the City Comptroller's office disclosed it would be auditing an Armored Car contract at the Transportation Department, which had covered the collection of coins from millions of parking meters in the City before Cosmopolitan. The city Comptroller's office wanted to determine why the city declined to renew a contract at a rate of 39.3 cents per meter and instead signed with a second company at a rate of 44 cents a meter. The second company had no previous experience in the collection of parking meters or in the collection of revenue. The spotlight was on the contract awarded to our employer.

Cosmopolitan responded by firing six of our co-workers-- the Bronx Boys. Cosmopolitan claimed they had evidence of theft from the Bronx meters. No evidence was shared to prove such allegations. The Amsterdam News ran a front-page article describing firings as retaliation to discredit the whistle blowers.

As if we did not have enough drama, New York City was hit by a major hurricane, a real punch-packing, tough hurricane. Such weather conditions were extremely atrocious, but still we were all ordered out to collect the parking meters. Reluctantly we went out in what was projected to be 100-mile-per-hour winds. Our vehicles were rocked fiercely by the strong winds, but our guys attempted to collect the money. A lot of debris was flying. Cosmopolitan said that it could not stop any collection of the meters until the city called it off.

This was again one of those painful moments, where I found it almost unbearable to see my co-workers whom I loved and respected out there enduring such injury and disregard for their safety. Because I was a driver, I was slightly removed from the cutting edge in the van. But outside, moving from meter to meter, being driven by some "I'm tough" instinct, passed on from generation to generation, with a frown on their face, and a forceful step in their walk, *wop-wop-wssh-waam* and an occasional scream *Baya!* They dodged flying trashcans and limbs, symbolic of the fragments in their lives, shattered dreams blown apart and scattered among the rubble, the weather but a reminder of all that was collapsing around them. My co-workers were determined to be an exception.

At some point, it became ridiculous. I called in our circumstances: "This is Richard to base. I'm sure the people of New York City will understand why we are unable to retrieve these badly needed funds for the city's budget today." "This is Richard to base: We are dedicated to make every effort to do our part to keep this city running, with maximum productivity. We are giving the best years of our life to retrieve the money from these blood stained meters." "This is Richard to base . . . "

While we were in the eye of the hurricane, our collection effort was finally called off and everyone was recalled. We definitely saw this as retaliation by our employer and the Department of Transportation. Meanwhile, there were rumors that Cosmopolitan management was going to come up with a proposal to our union leadership for a career ladder.

On legal advice, we filed complaints with the State Division of Human Rights in Harlem against Cosmopolitan. We were slow in going to visit elected officials and community leaders but did so. Sometimes we got a response, sometimes not; sometimes we met with assistants.

We did notice that Cosmopolitan and people from the Department of Transportation were following us as we went on our daily routines. We received a memo informing us that beginning on March 3rd, the city Department of Investigations and the Inspector General of the Department of Transportation would be watching meter collection activities, as well as making random stops and searches of collection vehicles. The memo instructed us to be very cooperative and to allow the officers to search vehicles for misappropriated and damaged city property, as well as other contraband. We were all stopped randomly while collecting the meters and lined up outside our vehicles while these officers searched them.

What an embarrassing spectacle this was with the public. We were publicly reduced to what appeared to be criminal suspects. We recorded names and badge numbers of the investigators that stop us.

The City kept its distance when it came to our conditions of work. Our work environment was considered just the normal order of business. No eyebrows will be raised over some cheap labor the city cleverly hides behind the scene and maintains for which ever contractor they want to give us to. You simply bring the money, provide the transportation and we will give you everything else you need. It is an exercise of business expertise perfected in the whorehouses of history.

Not once did any of these daily searches yield evidence of wrongdoing. At one point after being stopped, I began taking off my clothes in the street. It was as if they were performing a strip search. The investigators were very disturbed over how I portrayed the situation. They didn't like the image. I was standing on the street in my long johns, being very loud and boisterous over the search. I was attempting to dramatize how degrading the procedure was.

We were extremely humiliated by these events. While making a significant contribution to the City of New York on a daily basis, we were grossly underpaid, overworked in an unsafe situation, and on top of it we had to face yet another dreadful ordeal.

I was injured by a canister, which flew and hit me in the back. My doctor sent a letter to the company asking that they kindly implement the necessary measures to assure my comfort while driving any vehicles on the job. Cosmopolitan found that to be hilarious and the whole notice was ignored.

After the incident in which I took a lot of my clothes off and made a lot of noise about the search, I was threatened with termination. Cosmopolitan indicated that they were going to take punitive action against me. The guys quickly made it clear that to do such a thing would provoke tensions between Cosmopolitan and us around the collection of the parking meters. Cosmopolitan decided to back off and not take extreme action against me. I was warned.

We received a letter from our union leadership, from President Richard Costello to Cosmopolitan. He was protesting the termination of our six co-workers for theft. Mr. Costello explained that he was outraged about the unilateral type of discharges that have taken place, while no evidence was even shared. A date was set in a couple of months away for a hearing.

I was sent out to drive in Queens. Max was one of the collectors. I was double-parked waiting for the collectors. Max was almost at a point when he would need his canister and keys exchanged. A police officer on horseback rode up and ordered me to move. I told him that I was collecting the New York City parking meters. He replied that he didn't care what I was doing; I had to get this vehicle out of there. I was sure my appearance and that of the vehicle, had a lot to do with his insistence. At that moment, Max arrived and to protect the money exchange, I left the van to make the exchange. The police officer saw that the van had not moved, and returned, now angry, grabbing my arm. I hollered, "No please don't hit me. I haven't done anything." I made sure I didn't even wiggle.

Max also started hollering repeatedly, "Somebody look and witness this brutality! This is racism!" The police officer was shocked, and lowered his voice. The police finally let me go, and I calmed immediately, and he left. Max and I climbed in the van and started laughing like crazy. It was a spontaneous, effective response, but hardly a solution. That police officer would have never told a mail carrier or a PG&E person to move on. He was unaware that he was dealing with city servants. To him, we were just part of his everyday run-of-the-mill encounters with blacks and Latinos in a double-parked dilapidated vehicle.

It seemed as if a lot happened at once:

--We issued a press release that we, the parking meter collectors, had retained civil rights attorney C. Vernon Mason to sue the Cosmopolitan Care Corporation for wage discrimination and other unfair labor practices.

--We learned that a lot of keys, used to open the meters were broken in the parking meters during the time of the Hurricane. The company faced fines for each broken key. Cosmopolitan proposed they would give the entire workforce two hundred dollars for each week there were no keys broken. After discussions among ourselves in the morning meeting, we agreed to Cosmopolitan's proposal and were able to secure close to two thousand dollars fairly quickly.

--Cosmopolitan started to collaborate with the City openly; correspondence was being generated between them. We were hoping this was the balance we were looking for, to finally address some of our working condition issues.

--We learned that Cosmopolitan met with the new Commissioner and, reached out to our union leadership lawyer, Sol Bogon.

The city asked for the union as well as Cosmopolitan to submit recommendations, regarding the security of the vans and weather related work policy and rules. In addition, the city expresses interest concerning the issue of prevailing wages.

A meeting was set with our union leadership to begin discussing ways to work through these problems. Cosmopolitan initiated numerous conversations with us to explain what this was all about. We also heard that the Cosmopolitan contract with the City would be expiring sometime soon, though no date was mentioned.

Soon thereafter we were hit by two additional Cosmopolitan proposal/plans. One was a management proposal that we run the operation ourselves from the DOT Queens site, and we will self-select someone among us to be our overall plant manager. That person will be involved with us to supervise ourselves in the getting out in the morning, the collection of the parking meters and returning with our loads at the end of the day.

The second thing was a new Cosmopolitan managerial person. Management brought on a new person on their behalf by the name of Mr. G. He would sometimes carry a basketball under his arm. You could find him in the loading dock area bouncing that ball. Mr. G came across as being a very regular fellow that knew a great deal, especially sports. He started talking to people individually, he seemed very sympathetic to concerns we have. He suggested to the individuals he met with that if we worked with him, he will be able to make our situation better. Mr. G though friendly, never directly initiated any discussion with Jose or me about our issues. He also started to drop hints that we might want to think about hooking up with some other union; he had mentioned a Local 3 to one of the guys.

It had become a pattern of this management style to cleverly try to steer us into some particular direction, similar to how livestock are herded, instead of having an open, straight-up conversation about a problem and its solution.

Chapter 6

Controlling Our Work

We welcomed the opportunity to manage ourselves. The question is: Why was this happening at this moment in time?

We had arrived at a new crossroads. Cosmopolitan made the clearest statement thus far indicating they see The New York City Parking Meter Collectors as valuable. At least on a trial basis, Cosmopolitan was allowing us to direct ourselves and our scarce resources.

Nothing like this had ever been anticipated. It was as unpredictable as a breeze on a hot day, accompanied by a hummingbird under the watchful eye of a high-flying, spiraling hawk. We had to be careful.

Perhaps these jobs could have some long-term future for us, if we can only wrestle loose the resources to secure a safe and healthy work environment as well. We believed we could make things a little better for ourselves with the same amount of resources. So we were thrilled about this new idea, but not enough to surrender our objectives. We decided to pursue both. We had discussions among ourselves, and it was some real turning-the-corner thinking evolving about the possibilities at hand.

We elected Luis Cruz, who had some office experience under the previous contractor, to be our plant manager. Jose, Max, Luis and I would meet with management to work out the details. Luis will be the overall person to direct all activities for the collection of the meters from the Department of Transportation and he will also remain a member of our union organization. So we met with Fox and Mr. G and agreed that this would be on a trial basis.

Mr. Fox stated they hoped this way of operating would bring a better understanding between us. He said they agreed with a lot of what we were saying, but within the contract with the city, there was not enough money to improve working conditions. He also mentioned that he had family members that attacked him and quit speaking to him as a result of this conflict with us. Fox pointed out that there would be talks with the City and we would be involved. He sounded quite sincere. We reminded him of the dangers that we were facing, adding that with these increased dangers we must actively seek change.

So we started to be in charge of ourselves. The first day was not very different except that Luis was not in our meeting at the beginning. He was in the office paying attention to the assignments with Chapman. He joined us before our meeting ended. His focus was now on the meeting ending on time and us following the work rules. We all supported this. It was a good thing, of us having more of a stronger voice and more influence.

It was unclear as to what our next step could be or should be. We felt a certain awkwardness in this new arrangement of being more in charge of ourselves. Our challenge was no longer centered around stealing and disrespecting each other and the public, or on drugs and alcohol. Taken as a whole, we were in a strange situation, and in unfamiliar territory, as we were going through these re-adjustments into our new roles, clarifying who we were and where we were headed. Now more than ever, we needed help figuring this stuff out. Sensing that we have achieved a higher level of strength, we overreacted, and announce at our next meeting that "the buck stops with us and we were now in charge of ourselves."

We anticipated that Cosmopolitan management would be reaching out to us for our support to ensure that they were successful in securing a renewed city contract. So we need to redefine for ourselves our roles in terms of how we were operating now as a work force. All the management people moved off the premises and into a new location a mile away, except Chapman, who remained as an assistant to Luis.

With productivity as a top work goal, we had extensive discussion about how we were working. We talked about meters being skipped and people neglecting to collect certain meters. We encouraged everyone to make sure that all meters were collected on our routes.

We discussed a program to help with the special needs of some of the guys, particularly those with problems involving drugs or alcohol. I went home with Jaime, for example, and talked with his wife about his alcoholism, including the possibility of getting him into a treatment program. We dedicated some time in our meeting to discuss how to lift and handle the equipment to avoid back problems and other injuries.

The main issue was still in front of us: How would we continue to raise our issues and concerns about improving our working conditions. Sometimes we had to drag Luis out of the office to be at our morning meeting. We had him seriously commit to be at our meetings. As a result we successfully planned the work, balanced the workloads, and made sure the routes made sense as well as the team assignments.

One issue was that these contracts were always up every couple of years. There was no agreement that the new contractor has to acknowledge the union and any agreements we have with the contractor. To really secure these jobs, the contract needed to be longer with the city, and our lives needed to be a line item in the city budget. Our rights needed to be spelled out in these contracts to stabilize the workforce. We also discussed how to make sure the role Luis was playing could not be a trap of some sort that could be used to undermine the level of agreement among ourselves.

We were really getting the job done very well, management was happy with the outcome. The weather was still cold. Winter was coming to an end.

Wop-wop-wssh-waam! It felt great to have days in which I have two experienced collectors that race down the street. It was an extreme treat watching them. I guess one never got fully acclimated to not having any type of security and having our lives exposed to so much danger on a daily basis. But if there was one thing that can be really appreciated about the meters, it was watching two fast collectors racing.

I would also be listening to the radio, while catching a glimpse of the turn-of-the-century buildings that have also not changed. The oldies music and old buildings have the distant past in common, a memory sparked by unchanged sounds and sights, both a vivid connection to how far we have come as human beings. *Wop-wop-wssh-waam!*

Jose and I went to the grievance hearing over the termination of the Bronx boys concerning the alleged theft of monies from the parking meters. We had been unionized for over a year and for the first time management and us would sit across the table and hear the evidence presented and have the ability to argue over the merits of the case. Adding to our uneasiness was the fact that we never had received training about the grievance procedure; in fact we still never saw the contract. As a result, we simply handled everything from the standpoint of what we saw as fair, and this worked well for us. Cosmopolitan and our union leadership occasionally would try to tell us we were doing something in violation of the contract and we ignored them.

But here we were. It was our first time at the union headquarters in New Jersey. The union staff, Pablo and Richie told us what to expect at the hearing just moments before we moved into the hearing room.

The union asked for evidence of anything that had taken place. Mr. G. was there on behalf of Cosmopolitan, as well as a city inspector whom we knew and referred to as Inspector Gadget because of all the key and meter paraphernalia he had dangling around his waist.

The inspector said the city had started "salting" the meters beginning in May, 1985. This was a process in which they put special coins in the meters, with stuff on them not detectable by the eye. When the coins come back in the canisters they were counted, and if all of the special coins were not there, it was assumed that someone has been tampering with meters. The city inspector said he had salted 24 meters, and that five coins could not be found. There was some discussion that the coins could have been affected by rain rinsing them. Months later, after salting the 24, the city said a big area of the Bronx had been salted, and coins were recovered from 477 of 634 meters. The inspector said he had seen Hector, the collector, appearing to remove something from one of the meters, but that he had not approached the collector.

The city never could quite address the issue of other people having access to the meters other than the collectors. The city lacked a firm explanation for the coin disappearance. They even waited six months after the first suspicious salting results, before doing it again. It was brought out repeatedly that the people who service and repair the meters have access to the keys. In addition canisters sit on the loading dock, quite often unsupervised back at the Department of Transportation.

So the city could not really substantiate that the collectors had taken the coins. Quite frankly, we were thinking Cosmopolitan and the city had made this all up, in an effort to taint and scare us from going down the track we were headed in. But what alternatives do we have. Were we supposed to wait until one of us would be killed?

Cosmopolitan ultimately offered to pay the Bronx boys several thousand dollars each not to return to work. The Bronx boys decided to take the money. Jose and I could not make a different judgment. They said they needed the money. Right and wrong was buried somehow beneath the coating of the deal. We grudgingly hugged and said our farewells. Jose and I knew they were really our fallen coworkers and in that sense, true casualties. It was quite distressing. The city and Cosmopolitan had just saved face and gotten rid of a financial burden that could have potentially cost more.

At our morning meeting, we reviewed the case. Some were quite disturbed that the Bronx boys had taken the deal offered to them. It was felt that we needed to expose the retaliation and intimidating pressure that was being placed on us.

It was also brought to our attention that some small theft was taking place from a meter with a missing coin box, where the coins fell to the ground when you open the meter. We had yet another, lengthy discussion about how we must leave the money alone in the parking meters, and how it would jeopardize all the objectives we were attempting to achieve. We had to be prepared to explain the logic of our point of view over and over, because some of us were slower than others to get the message.

On a good note, going to church was on our agenda. Invites were being extended to everyone. A couple of guys argue that we should use less profanity when we speak. With the exception of the injuries, people were looking fit from all the various exercise programs, spending time at home with our families and not running around. Different families send special sweets to all of us occasionally, and express their gratitude at every chance they get.

Cosmopolitan initiated dialogue with the City to change their contract agreement, and asked for more money from the city to address our working condition concerns. It was our understanding that Cosmopolitan ultimately was told by the city, that the company would have to foot the bill of any additional cost and that the contract was more than enough to accommodate issues with the workforce.

We believed that Cosmopolitan knew from the very beginning that the City was going to take such a position. Cosmopolitan and also the City were going through the motions, since we have made public complaints. Everyone needed to show that a meeting took place and our concerns have been addressed through some formality. And so, now for the record, having responded to the business practice challenge, the city and Cosmopolitan could move on. There had been some semblance of an inquiry, going through the motions of taking necessary steps to preserve business as usual. Cosmopolitan had a contract with the City that involved millions and they were not about to voluntarily make any adjustments in the amount of income they were getting in order to accommodate the cheap labor side of the agreement. That was apparent.

In looking at the arithmetic, if you took the dilapidated vans, maintenance and gas, our clothing, salary and benefits, bond insurance, added the total cost of everything; to conduct our work and maintain us, everything would be paid for in less than one weeks work annually. The other 51 weeks (minus the 1.4 million plus the forty four cents times 66,000 meters that the contractor gets) goes into the city coffers each week. The city and the contractor clearly could meet more of our needs and decided not to do so.

Luis was handling his position very well. We were running the site in a positive way and better than it had ever been managed. We also knew we have to be very careful not to be lulled into paralysis by this new relationship we have with management. We had to remain mindful that neither the employer nor the city was addressing the critical issues. We have achieved important recognition from the employer, which indicates we really know how to run the operation ourselves. The operation ran smoother if we were holding ourselves accountable for getting the work done.

And of course, the arrangement had significant savings for Cosmopolitan Care Corp. Another important issue for the city and Cosmopolitan was the fact the workers knew the collection contract was linked to the city's big corruption scandal, and we were not as invisible as initially anticipated.

It must be said, our work environment was totally different than it had been. Our satisfaction was much better and it was mainly based on the cooperation and trust that we have achieved with each other. It has become so clear to us that our working relationship was an important engine of the workplace and our families. Everyone recognizes this achievement as being very special.

The other reality was that I was standing alongside my vehicle with the door open urinating; attempting to relieve myself of the pain I have been holding for some time. It served to illustrate just how fundamental our issues remained. We did not have a place to go to the restroom, and my appearance as a public servant actually discouraged the public from making such accommodations. We collected the millions of dollars that were used to service the city. Why was it so difficult to get the appreciation?

What made us so confident the public would be sympathetic to our plight? Maybe the public would see this arrangement of our lives being vulnerable, as the natural order of business. It occurred to me that we were exhibiting some real genuine trust and belief in people, in thinking that the public would do the right thing if given a chance to weigh in on our behalf. What trusting, genuine Americans my co-workers were, with a deep sense that our public is governed by a sense of doing the right thing. I could not believe us when I think about it. Underneath it all, we felt we were truly people advancing the belief of a precious democracy that profoundly distinguishes us from an antiquated past and numerous developing nations.

Wop-wop-wssh-waam, aroused by the spirit that we created among ourselves, from meter to meter, collecting the money for New York City and rising above our material conditions to take pride in the work that we performed for the people. And though our injured bodies were callused, bruised, and our flesh torn, we were proud and people could see it.

We enthusiastically repaired the carts that carry the canisters right in the street, taking money from our own pockets, to fix a wheel or use wire to secure the cart, so that we can get the job done, and never being reimbursed. Invisible in many ways to the public, who never notice how we were dressed, or the dilapidated vehicles we jumped in and out of. Our aches and pains were silently buried within the fabric of New York City.

We worked among the public, pulling an often unwieldy, broken and heavy cart. Often because of the honor of having an important job, we concealed it. The collector dragged that cart with a smile and an encouraged step, and though we were all crowded into a vehicle that did not even have enough seats for everyone. Yes we were somebody, we said, and to verify this fact, we would keep on pushing.

We finally had a few thousand dollars saved because we have not broken any keys into the parking meters. That was the agreement that we have with the employer that they would give us two hundred dollars every week that no keys were broken in the meters.

"The shop floor is now open," was the shout. The atmosphere was such a big improvement from what it had been back in the winter of 1984. We had a coffee pot going now with hot coffee for everyone. We had doughnuts for everyone, and often pastries being sent from family members. We had a room we met in every morning. We had a regular agenda that we adhere to. We had accountability among ourselves, and we constantly worked to achieve goals and objectives that stem from a plan. We had become a true union organization.

In this Reagan era of reverse discrimination claims, liberal whites and people of color were finding it increasingly difficult to act in concert. So we were learning that our jobs were at the mercy of particular social dynamics, in which people of color were convinced that whites were not equally horrified by racism, while whites don't believe this is the case. This was very new for us to be thinking and talking about the balance of different sectors in our city.

Often our instincts and hopes were at odds with each other, and we were often schizophrenic in our approach. Our instincts told us we could not trust our Employer and the City. Yet we expected them to allow us to have a decent life collecting the meters. In any event, our survival was dependent on us bringing attention to our issues and getting support. So the question was what specifically might we do?

The issue of South Africa and apartheid was in the news. A march was planned from the UN to Central Park, where a protest rally would take place. We agreed we would participate, involving our families and having a picnic in the park afterwards. We decided we would make a big banner that says who we were. We would have parking meter collector T-shirts that we could sell. We would make signs, bring food and have a good time. Clearly we were inspired.

We wanted people to commit to attend; indeed, we decided that there should be consequences if people committed themselves and failed to show up without a valid explanation. Someone said that if anyone failed to show up, they would get their ass kicked, which we all endorsed.

One of the guys knew someone with old silk-screening equipment who could create the banner and T-shirts if we helped do the work. A few of us agreed to create a graphic and a slogan and to help him to make the T-shirts. As instructed we brought

File photo The City Sun, now closed/David Vita, photographer

Parking Meter Collectors marched to Central Park, 1986.

him a silkscreen-ready negative, and started running our shirts through the process. It was slow, especially because we were new at it, but finally, we got it going. By two or three in the morning the banner was complete, but the shirts took another full day. It was exhausting and nauseating because of the fumes involved. But showing off the results drew a glow of approval; we had a banner 30 feet long and five feet high. We were all deeply excited about participating on the following Saturday.

Wop-wop-wssh-waam, was the sound of the parking meter collectors moving through the streets. All the windows were down in the vehicle. Caressed by warmth, the air was fresh and filled with a harsh yet sweet aroma that joggled my mind.

Luis Sandoz and Angel Pagan were with me this day. So Pagan's hand was bleeding all over the meters and the keys. When it was warm, it was difficult to wear gloves to collect the meters because your hands get hot and sweat so much. Your hands have to get adjusted to not wearing gloves while collecting. Pagan had not developed the proper callouses. We managed to get a bandage for him and made it through the day as fast as we could. Pagan would need the weekend to repair his hand or he would not be able to collect. Pagan was at the beginning of injuries that could have a lifelong impact.

We passed out the T-shirts to everyone and we finalized our division of labor for the event. Our plan was to caravan into the city from the DOT. The next morning, we had 34 vehicles full of friends and family. We congregated at the assembly site with our signs, which we were still preparing with markers, while we waited to begin the march. We had our T-shirts, we spread our banner; we were a significant contingent--The New York City parking meter collectors, "Parking Meter Collectors against Apartheid!" As we moved through the streets in front of the cameras, there were reporters who came up to interview us. We marched and chanted. We raised our voices high and blew our whistles. We made up chants condemning the existence of apartheid in South Africa.

At least ninety thousand people attended. The event strengthened our confidence that people care about each other. It reinforced our belief in the potential to gain the type of support we needed. We now knew that real support did exist. All these people came together to say that racial discrimination in another continent had to stop. Yes, all these people had that level of concern for their fellow human beings. What a lesson today's event was for the parking meter collectors. We met our goal, establishing our presence and we sold all of our t-shirts. In addition a big picture of us came out in The City Sun newspaper. We proudly placed the banner on the wall of our meeting room and it would become the background of all our future meetings.

But three people had not showed or called. The mood in the air was that they had an ass-whipping coming, based on the decision that we all had made. So being the leaders the responsibility fell on Jose, Max, Luis, and me to take the lead. We located them one at a time and hit each hard on the chest and arms, though less for the eldest.

The decision that everyone made had been carried out. By the next day we learned that one of the three had an uncle who was a police officer, who came to the DOT to inquire about his nephew and the reason for the altercation. We held our meeting the following morning and of course this whole situation had now begun to overwhelm us. Jose, Luis, Max and I stood firmly behind what we had all agreed to do. The three involved did not attend.

The atmosphere had flipped, and now was not one of great support for the action that had taken place. As we went out to collect the meters, there was discussion among us. The collectors felt that this action shouldn't have been taken against our co-workers. They said that we needed to find better ways to resolve our problems than to get physical with each other. Everyone appeared distressed; we had taken such a successful weekend and turned it into a successful mess.

It was apparent to everyone that this had to be addressed and stopped. And so at our meeting we decided that violence among ourselves was not a good idea to use under no circumstances. We decided that we would never put our hands on each other. We offered our deepest apologies to the three people we had committed this injury against. They all accepted our apologies. It once again allowed the smiles to return to our faces. The way we looked at each other always said much more than anyone could ever say in words.

Amazingly, we thought of ourselves as being tough guys. While deep down inside we were simply working people, overcoming some weary parts of our roots, trying to get along, wanting peace, respect and dignity. If given the choice, we would certainly make the right decisions. But if we made the wrong decision, there was evidence that we will make the effort to correct our mistakes, and ultimately move in the proper direction.

We had just gotten a lesson about dos and don'ts, and how we needed to be more careful in our approach to handling conflict about ourselves. Many of us came from backgrounds that did not give us a lot of experience resolving conflict in a good way, and so the toolbox was limited, forcing us to operate mostly in one gear. We were now learning about more options and the need to have greater flexibility. There was a time to be strict, a time to accommodate, a time to show compassion and love to those around us to be able to move forward, but never should there be a time for violence against each other.

We brought attention back to our outreach effort, getting the word out to elected officials and community leaders about our plight. We reviewed our talking points, and got back into the streets in the evenings and whenever we have time to meet with leaders. There was a long list of reporters, clergy and community leaders. We filmed our trucks and co-workers, talking about working conditions, including me, after I had been injured by a flying canister.

I returned to work, and found out I needed to finish filling out the proper paper work for workers' compensation. I learned that Cosmopolitan was going to be contesting my right to workers' compensation. I was somewhat disturbed when I learned of this. After all the hard work and dedication, I am rewarded with them contesting an injury that I received on the job, an injury that would be with me probably for the rest of my life. This was a difficult pill to swallow. In our morning meeting, discussion turned to the many other injuries that people had encountered. My injury certainly had to stand in line on a long list of injuries endured by my coworkers. This topic was just left hanging and unresolved.

Surprisingly, we had come out of our last internal conflict even more united, and now with one hundred percent, everyone was willing to participate and make their presence felt in our activities. What united us is good, what divides us is bad, was the thinking. The main thing was that we could not operate as if we had given up on one another and that the only way was a carrot or a stick approach. At all cost, we had to avoid us treating one another in the same condescending way many employers treated us.

Chapter 7

We Can't Do It Alone

The keys opened the meters with less resistance and everything was smoother during the warm months.

But then there was the issue of no air conditioning. We were moving into the time of year when we had to contend with the smothering afternoon heat in the van. It was as if we were sitting under the hood with our seats right on top of the engine. You could see the vapors from the heat, caused by the metal van and canisters consuming scorching temperatures and becoming damp with moisture. Everyone got accustomed to being drenched in their seats during the warm months – still, it was much preferred to the cold.

Our health and safety issues were not the priority they should have been, even with supportive news articles. Over the last year we believe we took emergency steps that avoided us being robbed at least a dozen times after observing suspicious activity, and there have been several unavoidable attacks against us, while we were collecting, the latest being some guy with a knife going after Jose Aponte while he was exchanging canisters and keys with a collector. The guy wanted to take the van. He was unable to get close to Jose and eventually just ran off. He was described as being one of the increased sightings, those "night of the living dead" flesh-eating characters.

Unfortunately, we were not getting appropriate attention regarding our plight, and our claims concerning how the parking meter contract was awarded. We had not gotten the attention of the city to intervene, to create laws that will protect and safeguard us. Yet we pressed on.

We came across a New York Times article detailing the growth of parking meter revenue since the first installation in 1935, and that traditional meters were starting to give way to electronic alternatives. Two parking meter companies build virtually all meters - Duncan and POM Meter Company; together they had 5.5 million regular meters in 47 countries. According to the article, New York City's 66,000 parking meters was the world's highest concentration. Another article discussed the electronic parking meter that New York was about to start installing, complete with battery power, a microcomputer and with auditing ability that could be installed inside any meters iron frame. A third article said New York's meters fill up almost as fast as they could be emptied, and the city planners were studying alternative meters, to use credit cards and even voucher systems that would basically do away with the current meter system all together.

Mayor Koch was a quoted proponent of new meters, saying, "The people that collect the money out of the parking meters looked as if they were going to get hernias." Newer machines could be emptied fewer times for higher prices. The article projected that parking meters would start disappearing for newer technology.

This was the first comment, and a one-liner at that, by the mayor about us, "the people who collect the money," in support of parking meter technology, jokingly and with little regard for the life-threatening dangers that we faced. This simple example exposed how the tradition and custom of cheap labor can overshadow our judgment in New York City and hardly raising an eyebrow from anyone else.

* * *

My co-workers and I raised questions about the future of this work. We wondered what new skills we would need. We discussed how we might ensure that we would not get thrown away, injured, discarded and replaced. Perhaps we could get subsidies to take classes. But clearly we have to get more attention on our situation, yes more appropriate attention.

Jose, his brother Angelo, Max and I attended a planning meeting with Vernon, our lawyer, for a forum on New York's future issues. We were asked to present testimony from our co-workers and to assist with the distribution of posters for the event. They would allow us to sell T-shirts as well. A couple of the planning participants said our work conditions were symptomatic of that faced by others. We report back to our morning meeting at the shop. People were quite receptive to the idea of us all going to this forum, which was entitled "The Other New York." We thought the title reflected our relationship to a city that found us invisible, and part of this massive group that public opinion simply steps around.

So we talked about being able to get T-shirts made up again, but this time with work done by someone who knew how to make them without our help. We located a company. All we had to do was give them the design. We took the design we have from the previous T-shirt and changed it to say: "Parking Meter Collectors Against Injustice," We had the picture of an expired parking meter in the center with chains busting loose. We made the time on the parking meter correspond with the date of the event. We had a few different colors of these T-shirts in various sizes.

We had not received any money recently from management from keys not being broken. We had just ceased to monitor this whole process of broken keys. In checking we found out there have been occasional keys broken. Our heads were in a whole different direction now, absorbed into the pulse of resolving our dilemma, throbbing deep within our greatest hopes.

Overall, there were so many real signs of improvement. There was an effort to bring things up in a sensitive way. Everyone was quite serious about our activities. Even those that were having problems that could jeopardize what we were doing, were also making it a point to acknowledge shortcomings and to assure us they got the message and will be getting it together. This was an important development.

It was important that speaking up at all these morning meetings had dramatically improved everyone's ability to communicate. We all supported Jose in his role to chair the meetings and he had really grown into this role. When we first started meeting as a group, most of us were always nervous and had difficulty speaking up. We were not accustomed to speaking before a group, let alone as many as 60 people. Now we were relaxed about speaking and some of us, like me, started talking too much in meetings.

This achievement by the guys started to manifest itself in other parts of our lives, at home and in our communities. We saw families getting stronger, and the evidence of more civic activity. Our families to a large extent showed their appreciation whenever they could and showered us with respect.

There was lots of enthusiasm in preparation for this next event. We acquired leaflets and posters from the organizers of the event, and gave them out to all our vehicles. There were approximately 10 to 12 vehicles now that go out every day, and there were approximately 40 regular parking meter collectors. In addition, there was now a much smaller group we were grooming, and who did not go out every day, depending on the amount of injuries or sick calls. Luis was working with us to ensure this group did not become a problem. We were careful not to become a clique. We defended any new person just as much as we defended any old one.

The drivers were making sure that the leaflets were placed on vehicles in the collection areas. I would secure the vehicle while the collectors were out on both sides of the parking lot, which gave me a chance to distribute leaflets; we all kept an eye on the vehicle, otherwise we didn't do it. Time was very idle for the driver in the parking lot, because I was mostly stationary and it took time for the collectors to move all around the meters. The driver was very centrally located. It was easy to select a small area and move the vehicle up, lock it and keep an eye on the vehicle and at the same time, the collectors. The problem was there was no security for the revenue, aside from the physical presence of some raggedy dressed driver with a two-way radio hook up. We have been conducting our own in-service on how to take care of ourselves and protect the revenue we carry. The city and Cosmopolitan never did this.

There was no written procedure about this from the city and Cosmopolitan. The only things that existed were what we wrote and shared among ourselves. We were ten thousand times more concerned about this issue than anyone else.

Finally one day, a week or so before the community forum, we learned that the city inspector had observed me distributing a leaflet in a parking lot, and reported it to the Department of Transportation and they were planning to take action. The person could have said they saw me distributing a lot I suppose, but they said they saw me distributing one leaflet. The Inspector General had gotten involved and was considering my termination. Cosmopolitan contacted me, and management indicated that they would try to do something to prevent this from happening, but it was out of their hands. At some point they say it appears there was nothing they could do and that it looked like my termination was going to happen.

We had our meeting and this news was not received well at all. The guys made it really clear that we would not collect any money out of the meters if they attempted to terminate me. It felt good to see my co-workers rally to my defense. While at the same time, I don't want anything bad to happen to them either. It was an awkward moment, what do I say. I have to conclude that the city's judgment in this matter has everything to do with how they have chosen to respond to the claims that we have been raising for the last two years. We saw the city's rigid position as an effort to use any excuse to put us in our place, which was to take issue with our continued campaign and silence us. Clearly what we were doing and achieving was not appreciated. If anything this attempt, gave us more encouragement to be successful at the upcoming forum.

Our T-shirts were ready and we had commitments from all the guys to be at the Forum. The Friday before the event, management had not taken action against me. The city has said informally to others that this was going to happen and Cosmopolitan could not do anything about it.

We had not heard from our union officials in a while and at this point we were not disturbed by this at all. Hopefully, the members of this union in other locations will someday quit sitting back and waiting on someone to take better care of them, and make the organization operate the way that it should. In the scheme of things, these leaders could do very little that we cannot achieve ourselves.

We prepared our testimonies. Everyone has written his presentation. We speak with Vernon's clerical staff and they help us with the editing. We were ready to go.

There was going to be a big, high profile panel comprised of Congressman Charles Rangel, members of the Assembly, Senators, City Council members, Bruce Wright from the New York's Supreme Court, Gil Noble, Bill Tatum of the Amsterdam News, William Kustler, Center for Constitutional Rights, Norman Segal from the American Civil Liberties Union, David Dinkins, Manhattan Borough President, Jim Webb from the Coalition of Black Trade Unionist and more.

This was quite an impressive panel and forum, and the parking meter collectors come out in force. We were all here. Topics range from education to probation, housing, policing and courts. There were so many people whose lives were being discarded as if the legal institutions have no meaningful, effective mission. All these people were in the same situation as we are, from young to elderly.

It doesn't matter if you are in a classroom, it doesn't matter if you are a low- to middle-income tenant, on probation for committing a crime. It doesn't matter if you are in jobs like the parking meter collectors, resources to correct these problems are directed away from you, and it was carried out quietly, with hardly a peep from anyone.

The victims don't even communicate to each other about what to do; everyone suffers separately and then feels bad they can't do better. Yet these are our parents, our sisters and brothers, our children, our neighbors who suffer and rarely have a voice like today, who operate as though they have given up and everything was just as it should be.

It was finally our turn to come up and speak. Our lawyer opened up by making some preliminary comments about us. He stated that the parking meter collectors are the brothers who go out at five o'clock in the morning and collect all of the 60 million a year out of those parking meters and yet they are paid literally slave wages for doing that; they got broken down trucks, they will tell you from their own experience what their situation is. Bruce Richard will tell you that as a result of participating in this forum, passing out flyers and announcing this forum, he was being terminated. Now I said that to you because we have to understand that as James Baldwin said "we have to come together because if they're coming for me in the morning, they will definitely be coming for you in the afternoon. We are going to let folks know that they are not going to get anybody when you come in the morning or the afternoon.

Vernon went on to mention how the Inspector General had gotten involved in me passing out a flyer, that the same people could not determine that the city was being ripped off for the last eight years under an arrogant man called Ed Koch but the Inspector General was involved with Bruce passing out a flyer. He warned that whoever was here from the city that we need to let them know, there will be no more money collected out of these meters, and that we are planning to march and demonstrate and do whatever was necessary to turn this around.

Someone also stated there were some 40,000 flyers passed out and that the parking meter collectors passed out most of those flyers. Norman Segal interrupted that he wanted us to call his office Monday morning at the New York Civil Liberties Union.

Luis Cruz spoke about subcontracting; he said the city uses these companies and they want us because we are cheap. He went on to say that: "the City doesn't want to do it themselves so what they do was they give these companies these contracts to use the minorities of New York City as cheap labor, that's one of the main issues we have to look into. These companies getting these contracts, especially like this company we work for Cosmopolitan, they don't have any prior experience whatsoever with meters or any type of security and they got this contract. That was something we will have to look into. We collect over 60 million a year for New York City; we walked 15 to 20 miles a day pushing 200 pounds of quarters all over the city with absolutely no type of security. The equipment they give us was these dilapidated vans, worth possibly $1,500 each. These vans have a braking problem because they were only designed for 2000 pounds and we are putting 10,000 pounds and up of money in these vans which caused a problem not only to us but also to the pedestrians on the streets when we could even brake properly. If we're going 55 miles an hour, there was no way these vans could stop. These vans only have 24 slots and 24 canisters; canisters are what we use to carry the money in. They give us up to 38 canisters, therefore we have a number of canisters that don't fit, and obviously they don't go into the slots. If we have an accident, these canisters were going to fly and hit somebody inside the van and perhaps kill them. These vans only accommodate two people. We literally have to get old cartons out of the street and put them in the van to be able to sit. It was ridiculous, that the city of New York allows these companies to use these dilapidated vehicles and equipment to collect all this money.

All we wanted was recognition, we want job security, and we are going to let all the meters overflow because if Bruce Richard was fired, we are not going to work. We work in all weather conditions, hurricane . . . We would like a pension, better salaries, some type of recognition of what we do, bringing a lot of money for New York City. We feel we are the best right now in the world collecting parking meters. Nobody else collects as much meters as New York City. We were doing a great service to New York City; we just wanted some recognition. "

Jose Aponte was called next; he stated, "the City of New York started subcontracting out in 1969. The first company to receive a contract was called Brinks. At that time the equipment was adequate, by this I mean better vans that were armored vehicles and better security. They were also receiving better wages, which at the time was $16.00 an hour, and doing one third of the work that we do now. After Brinks lost the contract to Wells Fargo, things stayed pretty much the same. Then came CDC and the season started to change, by this I mean that the contractor started to use cheap labor, which consisted of minorities. The wages dropped from $16 an hour to $8.00 an hour, also the work got heavier. Then CDC lost the contract to Armored Express. At this time the system was much the same, except for better vehicles. Then Armor Express lost the contract to Cosmopolitan Courier Service, which had no experience dealing with this type of work. Their specialty was with Building maintenance not with parking meters. Then the system went from bad to worse, by this I mean that the vans are used and in poor condition. Some of the vans have no locks, no third seat, no gate, no racks to prevent the canisters from moving and hurting someone. The carts that we use to push the canisters are broken down and worn out. Also our uniforms are second hand clothing and unfit to wear.

"Another thing was they cut our wages to five dollars an hour. Then one-third of the work force went up to $10 an hour due to two walk outs, some make as little as $5.00 an hour. Now we are in the same struggle with the company because the system hasn't changed. We are doing twice as much work than what was done ten years ago. I would also like to add that a lot of you folks out there, people who are here today, don't know what we go through when we are out there in the street. I'm sure that a lot of you have seen us and a lot of people say Boy, have you the easiest job in the world, but it was not. We walk from 15 to 20 miles a day. This creates wear and tear on our bodies. The bodies that you see right here and just about the entire work force have many injuries as a result of the type of work that we do. The wages, like I said $5.00 an hour. We got kids and we want to send them to college to get a better education and we can't even do that because the salary that we are making was not sufficient enough for us to send our kids to get a better education. Also, I want to say security wise, we don't have any kind of security. We carry $30,000 to $40,000 a day, each van with no security at all, like I said no locks. I mean, we are sitting ducks out there so that anybody could come at any given time and just take it from us and who knows they might even take our lives and what does this city say about that? Nothing! They come up with some suggestions, for what?

"With this crack out there now, we are sitting ducks and we want to prevent one of us from getting killed before it's too late. So that's what I'm trying to say, we need the help and support of everybody here and it ain't going to stop unless that happens. If Bruce gets fired, like I said, we are not going to go out there and work, we are going to stand together, we are going to die together, we are going to go all the way!"

Next was Max: "My name is Raphael Medina. Basically, I would like to speak about the dangerous and hazardous conditions that we work under. In New York City the drug rate is higher than ever, especially with this crack. It makes us more vulnerable than ever to get ripped off. The way it is right now, our lives are on the line everyday. We have absolutely no type of security. We would like to talk about an incident that happened on the 15th of August, Mr. Vargas, Mr. Rivera and I were inside our van on 162nd Street when a motorist spotted flames coming out from the engine. He screamed at us telling us to get out of the van that the van was on fire. I think that if it wasn't for that man that stopped to help us, we probably wouldn't be here right now. I don't know what it's going to take for the city of New York to do something about our conditions, but we are going to stand up and fight together." Dr. Donald Smith spoke up after Raphael, he said, "In the last few days we had received several frantic calls from Mayor Koch. His Black advisory committee is asking us what's going on. What is "The Other New York? The Inspector General thinks that what is going on with the parking meter collectors is detrimental and what's going on here is something that is very negative. We know we are getting very close don't we? We know that the enemy gets most frantic when he knows he is about to fall. So with that statement let me introduce the gentleman that we have been talking about, Bruce Richard."

So I was called up to speak, I opened up by thanking the distinguished panelist for allowing us to address the forum and the city, and to all the people that were present so that they could learn about the circumstances that we are dealing with. "I didn't know that when I answered a newspaper add two years ago, which spoke about lucrative jobs, good pay, benefits, that I was actually going to enter a night mare, I didn't realize that this kind of stuff was actually going on right here, we have a message here for you today, that message is to political leaders, community leaders "Don't let them kill us," They are trying to kill us. This economy is tight, things are getting hard, and they are looking for cheap labor. We were chosen to go out daily to put our lives on the line, just waiting for anybody to kill us over this money. We have no protection at all, like you heard the other brothers say here.

"Our message to the labor leaders if there are any people involved in labor "Don't let them kill us." We are fighting for our lives here, we need work, people are crying out for jobs and they know that, they know that people need jobs. There are 34 of us, and only 34 parking meter collectors that regularly collect all the parking meters in all five boroughs of New York City. You didn't know that, right? There are ten to fifteen extra ones that will replace us when we can't come to work, which is often, because let me tell you, after walking 15 to 20 miles a day, you are going to be off more often than you think you will be, that's for sure. It's no accident at all that we have been chosen to do this work. There are people in the New York City administration--I don't know if you people are aware of it, but these people believe that minorities are to be worked. That minorities can make more money than white folks can. That minorities are a good source of cheap labor, that minorities can just be worked into the ground. All you have to do is just keep them in their place, keep them in line and that's what they are trying to do to us, in fact, that's what they are doing to us. If you folks don't fight and defend and stand up with us, they are coming for you.

"You see, they are coming for the labor movement, you see Reagan's policy today, which can only be described as a policy of attack on the labor movement and the signal is out for all corporations and businesses to get that cheap labor, to drive over any type of organized labor, and to put these minorities back in their place. That's the signal. For those elected officials gathered here today, we are your constituency and if you don't stand up for us, they are coming for you as soon as they're finished with us, they will come for you. The parking meter collectors have been extremely frustrated with the sense of rejection to our efforts to obtain some justice. Our jobs are dangerous. This $30,000 that we are carrying around daily let me tell you, people are killing for less these days. Many of these people are desperately in need of work. Most of us have injuries in our fingers and in our hands; nobody has lasted on this job more than five years. After you do this work, after you collect these meters, for those numbers of years, walking up and down, the backbreaking work that we do, you are through as far as being a productive worker. Because your bones, your hands are destroyed, arthritis sets in at an accelerated pace, many of our co-workers can't even bend their fingers properly and it is just ridiculous to think that just ten years ago, these were jobs held by White workers who earned double the amount of money that we get and they did half the amount of work that we do today. What are we talking about?

"We had no choice but to get organized, let me tell you, they had us at each other's throat, competing with each other, they had a bonus system set up for us, by which whoever collected the more meters would get a few more pennies. So they had us competing with each other, no respect for one another and we had to turn all that around. You know what it is like to get $5 an hour and you are in a vehicle that's unsupervised and you have $30,000 in it? They are trying to corrupt our lives, that was what they were trying to do. They were trying to turn us into human beings without any kind of self-respect. We had to turn around and resist that corruption that's laying out there for us, we had to use these (referring to hands) for what we get, and these hands are bringing in $60 plus million dollars for the city of New York on a yearly basis. That money is supposed to help improve this city and what do we get? Nothing! We deserve better than this. What we have done among ourselves is a microcosm of what really needs to go on all over the city. We have gotten together, as small as we are.

"What we have done is to come together and this has to happen all over the city, where Blacks, Puerto Ricans, Dominicans, Jamaicans, people from the West Indies, all minorities need to get together because if we are not together, they will make examples out of us here. We don't have a lot of nice things to say here today, we are extremely upset… The city contracts out these parking meters to make a profit so the city gives the contracts to the lowest bidder, the lowest bidder by design, goes and gets this cheap labor for New York City. Like most of the country, when you talk about cheap labor in these big cities, you are referring to minorities. It is the people of color in these cities who are crying out to get a job, any job. Parking meter collectors have been cheated and abused, after several years of this type of work, we are burned out, and we are tired of it. We can't stand it anymore!

"The present administration has shown us no concern, we are going to Harrison Golden, the State Attorney Giuliani, and we have written letters, Mayor Koch is definitely aware of the situation that we are confronted with, where is this commitment to end discrimination and racism in the city? As far as we can see, there is none! We have displayed more concern about security and welfare in this city than the current administration has concerning these parking meters. We respect this city, we respect the work that we do because we know that we are making a contribution for the people in this city and this administration is driven toward making as much profit and money as it possibly can off of the backs of the minorities.

"All we want is the same amount of wages that they paid White folks 17 years ago. Yes, give us the cost of living increase too, we've got that coming! We are talking about 17 years ago. All we are asking is to give us the same amount of work, no more and no less. We're not crazy, they say we are lazy, that we want something for nothing, well they are wrong! All we want is the same amount of work that they had when White folks performed this job ten years ago. What do they think that we Black and Latinos are? Work horses or something, we are human beings and I tell you we are going to struggle, but we are going to demand that we be treated as human beings in this City. Thank you. One last thing, we have evidence right here on tape, we have everything, including equipment that we have been dealing with, we have it all right here, we have it all on tape and we are going to make it available, we will put the word out. This cannot be concealed and hidden from the public any longer because we know there are others in the city, in a different line of work that we don't know about, whose jobs are also subcontracted. We know they are trying to save money, they are trying to balance the budget on their backs, they are trying to use us as shock absorbers to this crisis in this city and the labor movement and the communities and everybody has got to come out and stand up, we are the most vulnerable sector in the work force, minorities in this city, when the crisis hits the city and you see the white folks out of jobs, just look at those of us on the bottom and examine the kind of jobs that we are doing, and forgive us for not going to college and getting a college degree, but is this the fate that we have to suffer for not going to college? I will tell you, we don't think so!

"We are human beings and we are going to fight for ourselves. They say that I was fired and let me tell you on this job I have done nothing more than talk about us standing up, being together, doing our work, not stealing those quarters. Let me tell you, what we have had to turn around is the tendency of this job to drive us towards drugs and alcohol and all those other negative outlets. We have turned that around, what we have done is taken a nightmare and we have turned it around on them. They may crack our heads come next week, they may kick our behinds, we may be out of work, and there is no telling what may happen. But we are going to stand up because we have dignity and pride. Thank you".

Members of the panel expressed support. They wanted to know more about my termination. I indicated that we are waiting on the paper work, but that the Inspector General had called the company and told them that he wanted me terminated.

We came out of this forum high as a kite, and we sold all our t-shirts as well. We talked about how good it would have been if we had a date scheduled for some other type of activity that we could have announced at this forum. But still we are all extremely energized by the reaction from the public to our situation.

The people there stood up and gave us a standing ovation. This was the first time we have really been given a voice and we have been able to tell our story to the public. We felt there are people out there who really did care about us and who are willing to come out and who are just as outraged as we thought they should be over what is going on with the parking meter collectors. We were really very happy to find people and to confirm that there is a caring public out there; this is the biggest thing for us that took place.

* * *

On the following Monday, there was a great deal of tension in the air. Everyone's composure was quite distorted, our eyes were sort of bugged out with serious, firm looks on our faces. There was such a vividly determine posture in the hearts and souls of everyone, and we all knew that at any moment, the employer could be making a big move against us.

We assessed our situation again, reaffirming that we cannot turn back. It was agreed by everyone that the incident with the flyer and the involvement of the Inspector General was a petty infraction and it's being used as an excuse. It's obvious there are much bigger issues involved.

We were told by Mr. Fox that the paper work has been typed up and it was being sent out in the next couple of days. We pulled together our committee, Jose, Luis Cruz, Max and me, and we went over to the management's office. Mr. Fox told us again, there was nothing he could do and that it was out of Cosmopolitan's hands, and within a few days they would need to carry out the decision. We went to our Tuesday morning meeting and decided we needed to act quickly.

At the forum, we created a phone list of community supporters that we will call in the event that we planned a demonstration. We passed that list out to coworkers to make those phone calls. We set our time and place for our action on the next day, giving management very little time to react and less chance of discovery.

We decided that we would come to work the following morning as usual, load our vehicles and in mass go to Manhattan for a demonstration in front of City Hall. We will schedule a press conference and we will place our dilapidated vehicles on exhibit so everyone can see the conditions we work under. We will come fully dressed in our uniforms for everyone to see. We will pull our carts out of the vehicles so everyone can see. We decide it's time and advantageous to bring our whole plight and struggle to a final head.

We believed we could not sustain our cohesiveness in any other way. It seems we have a better chance to win by taking some firm action, than to be waiting for something to happen to us, one by one, in some unforeseen circumstances, to be robbed and killed, or to be trapped by some vice, because of the circumstances under which we work. So we think there might be a chance for us to actually win this, if in fact we can gather some support and get some people to stand with us.

The action would be tomorrow, the place a Board of Estimates meeting, adjacent to City Hall and we could visit them as well.

I could not sleep all night. My thoughts raced, searching for thoughtful alternatives. Every direction that I considered was a gamble. I was so worried but yet determined. I closed my eyes and see the faces of my coworkers. I saw their families. I could not imagine continuing to sustain hope without taking the steps we were about to take.

Chapter 8

Fighting For Our Lives

The time had come to move in mass toward lower Manhattan. We all climbed into our vehicles and proceeded in that direction. We arrived in Manhattan with no incident. We kept our two-way radios on and there was very little communication between the base and ourselves. There was no suspicion from our employer at all that anything unusual is taking place on this day.

We arrived at South Street, and close to noon, we pulled our collection vans in front of City Hall. Our plant manager, Cruz, had held back at the Department Of Transportation, pretending to get calls from us indicating we were collecting the meters, and he has just arrived to join us. The time has arrived. We were the entire workforce, driving every single vehicle toward City Hall, to dramatize our determination to overcome this life of fear and preserve our integrity.

We assembled outside our vehicles and pulled our signs out; one of the guys starts to lead the chants he had helped prepare, along with all of us the night before: "No more can we take the city's big mistake". "We want protection, not rejection!" "We're sitting ducks with all these bucks", "For our Rights we will fight"; "We want justice, when do we want it –NOW!" "If the City feels no pity, we'll get down to the nitty-gritty." "Aches and Pains have gone too far, we're fed up and won't take no more." We shouted these chants all the way to the steps of City Hall.

We were greeted by a couple dozen or so legislators, community and religious leaders and reporters. We began our impromptu press conference, insisting that reporters look at the vehicles we have brought to the city, to showcase what we use to collect the money from NYC's parking meters. The vehicles were full of the canisters and everything that we carry the money in, so they could get a tangible idea of the conditions we have to work under. The press was taking pictures of our dilapidated vehicles, which were in unbelievable shape.

Then suddenly, we jumped into our vans and pull into the middle of the traffic filled street, moving toward the Brooklyn Bridge. The police unsuccessfully attempted to prevent this from happening, eventually surrounding us as we jumped out of the vehicles, and sat down in the middle of the street. Traffic came to a complete halt. A public bus arrived, the passengers were removed, and the police pulled us one by one off the street and into the bus to go to jail. The police attempted to retrieve the keys to the vans, but for most, they could not. A couple of the guys were designated to throw the keys over the bridge as a symbolic gesture.

The stalled vans were preventing traffic on the bridge, my dirty white van among them, with its dents and problems, the back door tied shut by rope and wire. I had a special relationship to that van. It has protected my co-workers and me from danger. Sometimes it had been almost human, and I had talked to it. I had not been robbed yet, and there it was now, looking so heroic yet detached, apart and distant from me, as we both were forms of equipment, in the process of being transported off, my eyes moist.

We were all placed in holding cells by police officers who actually sounded sympathetic. Within a few hours, we were all released and we assembled again at City Hall and chanted.

We went to the Board of Estimates meeting and demanded a meeting, and a few of us were escorted before members of the Board of Estimates who said they would consider our concerns and talk with the Department of Transportation.

We demanded protection on the job from robbery and theft, better equipment, a reduction in the work load, no more than 1,000 meters per van, health and pension benefits, we wanted to make sure that there were no repercussions for our job action, we wanted the same wages that had been in place 10 years prior for the white work force. We wanted the city to stop concealing itself behind the scenes, while we were victimized. We wanted these to be city jobs. We left with no commitment to address our concerns. We moved back into the streets, our entire workforce chanting.

In our morning meetings, we seemed to be many, but here, we were microscopic, a mere speck. People simply walked around us, ignoring our chants and what we had to say. It appeared as though we barely got the attention of anyone. Our chants were just among the many sounds of the hustle and the bustle and the horns and all the other ordinary noises of Manhattan smothering and muffling our voices, drowning us out.

We got a call at our lawyer's office from Cosmopolitan; they want to meet with us that night. Cosmopolitan said they were prepared to negotiate with our representatives, and us though later we learned they would see only the lawyer, Vernon. Vernon saw that as a very positive sign. Cosmopolitan wanted assurances that we would return to work the next morning while they considered our demands; they said they needed to talk with city officials. We discussed it as a group; it was the same old story. We decide we can't return to work without our demands being addressed.

The following morning, we reported to the Department of Transportation in Queens, expecting to set up our first picket line. However, Cosmopolitan had already recruited a lot of people to replace us, and they were already inside the loading dock.

It was quite strange, a Twilight Zone experience, observing all these new faces in our everyday work space, resembling and looking just like us in age, color and size. Perhaps our duplicates as the powerful seek to redirect the course of events, and since our replacements moved and looked so much like us, we wondered if our "sticking together" messages could resonate.

We began to tell the replacement workers about our mission, telling them that it was a trap and not to do it, saying, "Those are our jobs don't try to do our work" and "You should leave the building and join us."

A couple joined us, but the overwhelming majority ignored us. Some gave us the finger and shouted insults at us. The replacement workers insinuated verbally and non-verbally that we had lost out to their gain, that we were fools and they were going to do our work no matter what. We would later learn that replacement workers were also referred to as scabs, describing that ugly, hard, crusty substance on top of the wound that working people endure every day, giving a deceptive picture of the damage underneath the scab where the pain and suffering of working people fight toward progress in their lives.

The police came and insisted that we move away from the entrance, so the operation could be free of interference and business could transpire as usual. We remained in this distant, out-of-ear-and-sight location that the police had assigned us, but saw that no one had gone out to collect the meters. We knew Cosmopolitan would face daily fines of $30,000 or more.

We knew we were in for a fight, so we began getting ready. The plan was to prevent the replacement workers from collecting the meters by flattening the tires of the vehicles. A couple of guys were assigned to purchase good knives for this purpose. We broke ourselves into two groups in each borough; one group would search and locate the vehicles and the other group would flatten the tires. We had yet another smaller group of dispatchers operating from the New York Civil Liberties Union in midtown Manhattan that would receive the calls identifying the target areas and send us out to flatten tires. We all decided we would not go home at night. We will find alternative places to stay until this matter is resolved.

For the first several days we prevented collection of meters, and, in fact, it was almost fun. We would see them in the field studying maps attempting to understand where the meters were. The locaters would call this information into our makeshift war room and our dispatchers would take down the information. The action team included at least two people to cover both sides of the vehicle, and one had to call the war room every 30 minutes for location coordinates. They would be dispatched to the collection vehicle where, disguised as passers-by, they would flatten all four tires. By the time they would notice what happened we were already gone. They had to replace two of the tires, and then get the vehicle towed.

We hit them successfully in all of the boroughs. By the third day, Cosmopolitan had police riding in the vehicles. It did not detour us in the slightest. We continued to hit the vehicles even with the police presence. The police were not dedicated to the task of preventing people as determined as we were. Cosmopolitan still could not collect the meters.

A week passed. We got word from Chapman that the whole operation was a big mess. The replacement workers were trying to use maps that were not very accurate. Cosmopolitan had wanted to fire Chapman, he said, but decided to keep him on of course, since he was the only person that knows where the meters were located. He was clearly saddened by us not all being together, and we were too. Chapman was a very honest person and a wonderful human being. We all missed him. We didn't make any request of him. We all have much respect for

Chapman and didn't want to place him in an awkward situation. We know he identified with our concerns. He had also lived it every day.

We knew the fines were adding up for Cosmopolitan. We have been trying to hold meetings with the city to get them to intervene; it was not our intent to be an obstacle to the cities badly needed revenue. But the city was still taking the position that they were neutral in a labor dispute between Cosmopolitan Care and its employees.

In the meantime, we learned that our union leadership has been down at the loading dock of the Department of Transportation signing up the replacement workers to become members of the union. This was no surprise, but yet another indication that we were not only having a fight with our employer and the city, but also with our union leadership. We symbolically took the position that we would be represented by our own independent union and made our name officially, "The New York City Parking Meter Collectors."

The ILA union leadership sent word to Jose that they wanted to meet—this time in a Queens hotel. Our union president, Richard Costello Sr., and Secretary Treasurer Richard Costello Jr. were both there, as well as Sol Bogon, the union lawyer. We reserved our finger pointing and just listened. The union leadership had no alternatives to offer and very little if anything was suggested. They asked if we were ready to return to work. We said we would only if our demands were met. This union leadership clearly was not offering any direction. We saw them as just out on a day's hustle, protecting their financial interest through whatever means available to them.

* * *

I wondered why the leadership of a union would make such reckless decisions and how this behavior could be considered legitimate and tolerated among working people. I suppose in many ways we all display the same symptoms. Just as we parking meter collectors decided we were tired of our outcomes and that we needed to clean up our act, perhaps others could do the same, embracing a higher obligation.

What we learned was that the criminal element only existed in a very small fragment of the American labor movement, but it left an awful high profile scar, sensationalized by TV and serving its own interests, keeping working people feeling powerless, isolated and with no desire to find common ground among themselves.

In earlier days, big corporations openly hired private security companies as goons to beat or kill workers when they would try to stand up to their bosses. However in parts of the transportation industry, unionized workers decided to defend themselves and sought help from the criminal element, who were also tough and could effectively engage in violence. It was the kiss of death, two sides of the same coin, only one was legal and the other illegal. This was a marriage with imagery that working people have yet to clean up.

We suspected – there was no proof-- that a Cosmopolitan manager may have actually called the union leadership to set up this final meeting.

Meanwhile, we were without income. Some of us looked for jobs; because of community support, a cab service in Brooklyn agreed to allow some of us to be drivers. Most of us, however, kept on preventing collection from the meters, flattening tires every day.

Cosmopolitan had sent word that they were going to take us to court to collect over three hundred thousand dollars in damages for the vehicle tires. We were also taking legal action, seeking injunctions to prevent hiring of replacement workers and not bargaining in good faith with us over major health and safety issues. We went to court in Brooklyn and in Manhattan, but we received no relief. All of us received telegrams stating that we had been suspended.

On October 3 — a year to the day since we had met to form a circle and vowed not to steal from each other or the city -- we received a telegram informing us that we had been terminated. A year later and we were all fired. Just think, we said to one another, we could perhaps still be there disrespecting each other and stealing quarters.

I was part of the group that went out to flatten tires. Our observation was that the police were appearing to be a lot more alert; when we flattened the tires, the police would chase us. We did it so quickly that most of the time they would be caught off guard, and by the time they picked up the speed in the foot chase, we were gone, leaving four flat tires in their mist.

Of course, we hoped that because of the fines, continuing bad press and the legal pressure something would break in our favor soon. To our dismay, we eventually learned that the city had gotten involved -- unfortunately on behalf of Cosmopolitan Care Corporation and not us. The Department of Transportation suspended the fines and was giving as much leeway as Cosmopolitan needed to defeat us. There was one important remnant of the past that local city governments have always made clear: Avoid getting involved in the matters between a man and his property, between the slave and the slave master or the man and his wife. The dominance of one over the other was considered natural.

Now since business as usual was being tampered with, the city had decided to suspend important contractual obligations they otherwise would impose on the contractor. We sent groups to visit some of our elected officials again. We met with David Dinkins, and were considering how to block the city contract to Cosmopolitan. Bill Lynch suggested we bid ourselves on the contract. Others, including those in Ruth Messenger's office, wanted more information about possible city corruption rather than the labor dispute. Apparently, defense of the workers was perceived as risky.

It was the Reagan era, and not a good idea to find yourself on the side of workers. Unions were being scapegoated as being unreasonable, with decent salaries that hurt employer budgets. The public appeared to be reconsidering whether proper compensation for workers was a worthy objective. We needed all the help we could get, regardless of the focus; we cooperated with everyone. We gave as much information as we could about our experiences with this contractor.

Several weeks passed with us looking for income and Cosmopolitan still unable to fully collect the revenue. We met and decided that we would make one final push and spend the weekend disabling all the meters in New York City, jamming nails into the meters. But our lawyer, Vernon, stopped us, saying we would lose any leverage we had if we acted. Reluctantly, we agreed. Instead, he filed another set of legal arguments.

Meanwhile, we learned that S&D Maintenance Company, the meter repair outfit, had closed, laying off all their 100 employees. The city had withheld more than two million dollars in contracts because of Transportation Department audits. The company said they had cooperated with the probe and a shut down more than likely will cost the city millions of dollars in revenues. We also learned that the city had changed procedures for Cosmopolitan to collect the meters, reducing the number of required collections by half. We saw the city adjusting the required revenue to allow Cosmopolitan to resolve its dispute with us in a favorable manner for Cosmopolitan.

We had another demonstration-- at Gracie Mansion, home of Mayor Ed Koch. We raised our voices there along with community supporters because we were convinced that the Mayor knew all the players in this dirty game. Since our problems reflected the corruption crisis, it was clear to us the Mayor was looking the other way and finding it difficult to address our concerns.

Also, Anthony Ameruso, the Transportation Commissioner, was named the subject of investigation in the awarding of contracts to S&D Maintenance; it was Anthony Ameruso who awarded Cosmopolitan its contract.

If the city corruption investigation could just plunge deeper into the fabric of work relations in New York City, they would find us with our arms reaching out, the little people who do the work, invisible and unrecognized. Hello, here we are! We're fatalities also! Our hands are extended! Can you see us, can anyone hear us? We are important human beings also, so please pull us up!

Our legal activity had become quite important to keeping hope alive and things going. Our lawyer filed a civil suit in US District Court, calling for another injunction order against the employer. We were suing for nine million dollars in damages from the City and Cosmopolitan. There was one great cartoon in one of the city's newspapers, which showed police officers holding a blanket, being used to cover the parking meter scandal. We pushed forward, similar to how we had always worked daily going from meter to meter, not giving up hope. Surprisingly, the victory we were hoping for took on new dimensions and we accomplished things more significant than could ever have been imagined.

Chapter 9

Beyond The Storm

And so fast-forward six months: After weeks and months in combat, we had our showdown, taking our public plight to the steps of City Hall, blocking traffic, lying in the street, and going to jail, all in an effort to improve our job conditions. The parking meters were jammed all over the city for a short time, packed with quarters, keeping revenue from being collected. We were not proud of any harm brought on this city, but we also had to fight for our own cause. We were public servants, now unemployed, who tried to help maintain the city's infrastructure at bargain rates and under unhealthy conditions, threatening not only our lives, but our characters.

We were tomorrow's young men at our first real job, our vulnerability obvious, and by design we became part of a business plan to maximize short-term financial gains for a company and a city that resulted very much in a social molestation. We are continuing to press for justice in perhaps not always the best way, but it's the only way we know. We lost; we were out of our parking meter collection jobs.

Within a short time, most of the guys have found other jobs. It was apparent that none of us was going back to collecting meters. The main view of the guys was that it would be best not to return under the same circumstances. Still, it wouldn't be until some time had passed for an assessment of what had been learned.

In the months after the showdown, there were a lot of continuing developments:

For a fund-raiser, we assembled a basketball team made up of collectors. We played the WBLS radio station "Sure Shots." Tickets were sold in advance and at the door. The guys played exceptionally well, and though it was a very close game, we lost. Luis Cruz and Rangel Minaya had both played professional ball in the Dominican Republic and we had a few other skilled neighborhood ball players, like Jose Aponte. The proceeds were needed to help with our legal expenses.

There also was a dinner-reception held honoring the courage and sacrifice of the New York City Parking Meter Collectors and their families, at the Fort Green Senior Citizens Center in Brooklyn. All the guys and their families were together, and people who had become friends. This was the last time all the parking meter collectors would assemble. We are given plaques and certificates of appreciation. We not only had survived the ordeal but we rescued and strengthen our characters for an uncertain future.

Like dependent family members, we have all been tied into and responsible for each other's safety and well-being. Our expressions reminded me of sending a loved one off at the bus station, that while there might be a farewell smile, there also would be sadness associated with this particular good bye. We all gripped and hugged each other tightly to get that one last supportive embrace. There was no loud display of chatter coming from anyone, only the close whispers as we all sought to capture the special significance of this last moment together.

In less than a year of our firing, the entire replacement (scab) work force was arrested in October, 1987, charged with stealing as much as one million dollars. One news article said the replacement collectors were making regular trips to Atlantic City to cash in the quarters. The judge in the cases accepted guilty pleas, and said she would not impose jail terms if these defendants stayed out of trouble for a year.

Mayor Ed Koch apparently was upset by the ruling, and said that the city was a victim of a crime and that he had a right to appear in court to make a victim's impact statement. Koch added that he intended to do that himself to change the judge's mind, to impose jail sentences and to require restitution.

At the ILA union, Richard Costello Sr., president of Local 1964 and his son, Richard Costello Jr., the secretary-treasurer, were found shot to death in the New Jersey union headquarters less than three years later. The union president had been shot six times, and his son had been shot five times. Newspaper coverage suggested that the men had been victims of a turf battle between the Gambino and Genovese crime families. Richard Costello Sr. was described as an associate of Thomas Gambino, a leader of the Gambino family. The article also said that Richard Costello Sr., had helped the Gambino family take the 1,100 member union local away from the Genovese family five years earlier.

Anthony Ameruso, the previous head of the Department of Transportation, was convicted and serving weekends in Riker's Island for lying about the additional money he was making on the side with people doing business at the Department of Transportation, though there was no mayoral outburst about leniency there.

Michal Lazar, who had headed the Department of Transportation before Anthony Ameruso, also served a year in prison, reduced from three years.

Earl Caldwell of The (NY) Daily News, remarkably summarized it all in his article entitled "For Forty Whistle Blowers City Had Forty Winks," he said "that by the time they came to City Hall they were begging, they were pleading with anyone to just hear them out. The arguments they had were so strong, they believed they did not need anything else. There were about forty of them, they were not city employees, but they were working for the city. They were the guys collecting the money for the city. Some had been on the job three years; some five years, and a few others even longer. Some earned as little as $5 an hour and others as much as $10. But it wasn't money they were mostly concerned about, they were scared. They were among the first to see up close what the drug crack was doing to the city. They had people high on crack coming at them with knives because they had these canisters crammed with quarters. They had no protection. They had just old beat up vans, some so ragged that the doors wouldn't lock and that was the only refuge they had…

"So early in 1986, they came to City Hall, blowing the whistle, the forty guys who worked for Cosmopolitan Courier Corp. of Queens, which had the city contract to handle the parking meter collections… They spoke of the way crack was making the streets dangerous. Their bosses told them to just do their jobs. On the day they went to City Hall, they drove the old battered vans they used while collecting parking meter monies, but they got no hearing. They tried to make the most dramatic demonstration they could. They actually laid down in the street. Nobody even asked what was so wrong that it was prompting you to carry on like that? No elected official at City Hall that day took the time or the interest to talk to the folks who picked up the parking meters money. City Hall called the cops on them and they were all taken to jail. But that was not the end of the story; the collectors went on a wildcat strike. They belonged to local 1964 of the Longshoremen's Association. But their union gave them no backing. The city gave Cosmopolitan a wink and a nod, saying; get rid of them, and that's what happened. They fired the whole group of them and they brought in scabs.

"Yet, nobody in New York, which is supposed to be a union town, uttered a word in protest. So last week it came out that there had been looting of the parking meters money. And there was Mayor Koch and Transportation Commissioner Ralph

Sandler beating their chests, saying looks what we did; look how great we are. But they never mentioned the guys arrested were scabs and there would never have been a "rip off" had they listened to the workers who came to City Hall pleading to be heard. Bruce Richard was a leader of the fired workers. He had to leave New York. He couldn't find a job here, so he went to Philadelphia where he is working as a union organizer. "We were crying out for help," Richard said. "But we couldn't continue the way it was, our lives were in danger." Now the city has ended its contract with Cosmopolitan and has decided to make meter collectors city workers. That's what the fired workers suggested, but nobody would listen. "We really wanted those jobs," Bruce Richard said, all we said was that we wanted some protection."

Earl Caldwell of the Daily News hushed all debate. There were many others out there that are in predicaments similar to the parking meter collectors. It is a part of New York that is invisible, unnoticed, taken advantage of; it is "The Other New York."

A responsible city administration cannot justifiably conceal themselves along with the prestige and pride of the city's servants, behind unscrupulous contractors that pay bargain discount, poverty wages, and then set $30,000 in front of these same low wage earners every day and not have major problems. This was a business plan that involves placing a steak sandwich in front of starving people every day and walking away with the expectation that it will be untouched when you return every day. And so that's why the wages and conditions of work, extended to the all-white workforce 15 years prior made a whole lot more sense.

* * *

For me, this experience clarified my role as a human being, and taught me how important it is that I play a conscious role among my co-workers or community residents to achieve progress in a terrain that is so often stacked against working people. Before the parking meter experience, I felt awful that I had not figured my life out yet: Should I go back to school to attain a degree, or learn a trade that I had yet to decide on? It was a difficult place to be in, but I realized my value in the course of the parking meter job of just being an everyday working person. There's a void that is needed to be filled by people like me, right on the terrain of the everyday job that is vitally life saving and relevant.

Soon after the final farewell gathering of the parking meter collectors, I was able to get a job with the United Electrical Workers Union (The UE). This remains a legendary radical union that once had over a half a million workers, concentrated in large factories like General Electric and Westinghouse, before the infamous McCarthy period of the 1950's.

I arrived at the UE during the bottom out period of runaway shops taking production and jobs overseas. The UE was then down to 65,000 members. I was around during plant closures and the sadness associated with loss of jobs. I would find myself in bars, along with workers and staff drowning our tears. It was a devastating period for working people in this industry.

These locals once had been so large that they had a lot to say in their social environment and community life. It was a vivid reminder of what working people can achieve, though those artifacts and remains were about to be buried. I was a part of closing a union office near a GE plant in Pennsylvania that once employed over 30,000 employees. The shop leadership had aged and were quite distraught, as the dusty paraphernalia of UE political books and novels, radio scripts and cultural materials were being pulled out. The once powerful role of the union was becoming only a skeleton of small electrical appliance production shops in the area, though even some of the smaller shops were closing as well.

In the face of this reality and the defeat of the striking Air Traffic Controllers, a feature of the Reagan era, it was a surprise to me that there were very few shops that were internally organized as the parking meter guys had arranged. I did not realize what the national impact of worker defeat looked like and how it can graphically reflect the workers' perception of their relations with one another. Many of the workers remained too much of a shadow behind the union leadership. I couldn't figure out why so many workers were resigned to operate in this way, even though the union was largely democratic. I did not understand at the time that I was bumping up against the growing issue of employees' declining regard for each other, a symptom of the decline of labor unions, which had an impact on broader social issues from the workplace to community life. Enthusiastically, I saw an opportunity to assist the remaining workers achieve what we had accomplished among ourselves as parking meter collectors. I felt that I knew a lot about the ABCs of workers being in the worst place and being able to come together. However, I did not sufficiently appreciate how now accomplishing this from the outside would prove to be a skill that would take some time.

As a union staff person, every day was about efforts to organize the unorganized and support members in the unionized shops. I begin to translate my previous experience into a passionate message about workers building a strong relationship among themselves to achieve workplace objectives. My wife, Vicki, and I had adopted a baby girl, Maya, and they remained in Brooklyn, as I took up residence in Pennsylvania and commuted back and forth.

Within a short time, there were new positive dynamics in a few of the shops where I was assigned. Still, I got caught up in some of the union's internal conflict, and even into a physical confrontation with the District President, after what I perceived to be an incident of aggressive racism. I was wrong in taking part in this infraction and it really highlighted old baggage and the fact that I still had some rough edges to work on. I found an opportunity to seek an organizer's position with Local 1199 in New York City, representing health care workers.

Although the local usually only hired from within its ranks, I had somehow preserved a decent reputation or at least they were prepared to give me a second shot, and I was able to get the job. I was so excited about this opportunity to work for such a powerful organization and with so many people of color in leadership. 1199 was Dr. Martin Luther King's favorite union, and had such an important legacy of democratic unionism. I was given the greatest opportunity ever to work with others to advance worker rights and social progress objectives.

Local 1199 was also in the midst of an internal conflict, with the membership largely demoralized. There was a fairly new union leadership team that was committed to strengthening the democratic principles on which the union had been founded. My passion and way of working intersected well with the time and circumstances facing the organization. The leadership began to take notice of my early achievements, and I was soon offered leadership opportunities, becoming a vice president and soon thereafter an executive vice president as our organization grew in membership from 75,000 to 450,000 health care workers in six states, the largest local union in the world. It has been my work with the Parking Meter Collectors that has contributed to whatever asset I have become today.

In terms of some of the guys: Max also became an organizer for 1199 for a number of years, and later returned to the race track, where he stables, owns horses and races them throughout the East Coast for a living, bringing humanity to the horrible backstretch of the race track world. His son has become a well-known jockey. Jose Aponte became a religious minister, and he and his wife have a congregation in Orlando, Florida. Luis Cruz owns a successful trucking business in Florida, and the "Grandmaster" became a successful banker.

* * *

Never before in NY history, had the parking meter workforce been so cost effective. The workers brought in more revenue than ever and the operation was so inexpensively administered and maintained. This was an example of how a city can draw in maximum revenue and manage itself at low cost.

But an even greater development was taking place: the morale, the self- confidence and esteem of the entire workforce kept growing. The workers relationships among themselves also grew--through religion, physical exercise, culture, politics and community. At the heart of this transformation was people having restored confidence in themselves and others. They refrained from drug use, cut back on smoking and drinking. Co-workers felt better, looked better, enjoyed the presence of one another and gave each other support. Their families were grateful to see the change. Co-workers often visited each other's homes for dinner, where they would be showered with gratitude as families held greater hope about the future.

The meter collectors' primary accomplishment was not the improvement of wages and benefits or working conditions; but how they worked with each other to transform themselves.

The parking meter story did not end happily ever after. The Parking Meter Collectors did not have the supportive resources from the employer and society to sustain such activities. Aside from themselves, no one cared about such a workforce achievement. The fact was that the effort was driven by the collectors alone and with little contribution from anyone. But the collectors' experience proved uplifting; the workers learned to operate in a positive way among themselves, to have successful outcomes in their work, and to translate their work experience into social progress.

The protection on the job, benefits and wages were definitely important, but more valuable was workers going from distrust of their fellow human beings to confidence and commitment to each other; from unconcern about their personal health to creating an exercise program; from individualistic, less socially involved people to culturally involved, civically responsible people.

The workplace became a pivotal engine for enhancing social relations. The parking meter collectors made significant gains in terms of how the work was organized among themselves and in the relationship with the employer. By improving their relationships with each other, they realized greater success on and off the job.

When employees successfully overcome self-containment, we were in the best position to improve things. Employees can finally imagine the possibility of achieving and having resources that one cannot have as an individual, creating a future that could not be accomplished alone. Such examples are indispensable to America's workforce strategy.

Unfortunately, in this very advanced day and age, the workplace maintains the largest remaining bastion of servitude-like relations, where employees across America find their critical engagement restricted and still do not enjoy the basic right to sufficiently dialogue among themselves about the work they perform in common.

There is little emphasis placed on the fragile nature of employee relations, with virtually no acknowledgement, that employees do not adequately value work related interaction with each other. There is not even the slightest examination surrounding the lack of quality employee interaction and its impact on work outcomes, let alone its impact on broader community social relations. There are virtually no agreements that acknowledge anything new needs to happen regarding a space, or dedicated resources that specifically emphasize the quality of employee interaction regarding work. No attention is given to developing skills among employees to strengthen their collective necessity to run meetings among themselves, manage conflict among themselves, dialogue regarding critical data among themselves. There is virtually no data even dedicated to measure such important human activity.

In essence most U.S. employees are not allowed, and have never made agreements or commitments to each other regarding how they will more effectively work together, this being at the heart of a catastrophe, and why their remains gapping wounds within the employee experience that need to be prioritized for healing.

Employees find themselves inhibited in the production of goods and services, denied the right to bring new consciousness to the work environment, sending a signal of worthlessness to the people that are needed so badly to get things on track. Our society has been quite successful in promoting a standalone philosophy to its citizens, resulting in many placing little significance on finding common ground with their neighbors and those that they labor alongside every day. Yet people need each other to realize their full potential.

We have a crisis escalating the surface temperature at workplaces, having a devastating impact. Employees leave work demoralized, lacking the tools and resources necessary to address the fragmentation of their neighborhoods and communities. The dreadful work environment clarifies why, even though so many are without work, employees are far from thrilled to have a job. Employees are not sufficiently invested in the success of their workplace, even though their quality of life depends on it. It's a worthwhile objective to locate the passion that would have more people want to come to work and really value what they do.

Yet even though employees from the most subtle to the most explicit express daily dissatisfaction, our social order does not recognize the oxygen being siphoned from the atmosphere by today's management approach.

It's an evolving tragedy having to do with workplace relations and its powerful impact on the fitness of our nation. The workplace is not only vital to the production of goods and services but is also a place of significant social relations, a place to measure the maturity of our society. Not only should excellent outcomes in production be accomplished for business to thrive, but also it is critical that employers reverse the "disposable" approach to labor. Employees must be appreciated and valued in order to sustain long-term success. The absence of such appreciation is a dilemma for the US of crisis proportions. For too long, employers have been empowered to have absolute control over these crucial social relations in our society.

Customarily the management position relative to employees is one of extraordinary influence. Setting the right to hire and fire aside, management has say on all matters of flexibility with respect to work schedules. Management has say on a host of very important employee concerns such as sick time, vacation, all paid time off and all leave of absence approvals. Employees by far do not want to be regarded as a trouble maker or find themselves in disagreement with someone that has so much power over them. Employees never know what can happen in their lives and may need the flexibility of management.

However, employees cannot afford to not look toward each other for solutions, it's the missing most neglected priority and element of today's workplace. The relationship that employees have with each other is the most injured element of the labor/management process. Addressing this issue is most important to achieving workplace success. It's important to leverage every opportunity to increase employee capacity.

Employees have a catalyst role to play in improving how work is organized. Labor needs to create a caring environment for itself at the workplace, allowing wounds of separation to heal, producing a sense of belonging and commitment, instead of being dispersed by indifference.

It's critical that employees create a sense of fulfillment through problem-solving for themselves, enabling employees to have a greater sense of what they can achieve together. To do this, we have to first overcome the negative practices that foster poor social relations.

Though we may be casualties of injustice, this cannot lull us into not taking responsibility over our lives. It's crucial that employees overcome the belief that the legal system or any outside party should have sole responsibility to solve our problems for us.

The parking meter collectors had to be on a mission to turn the tide on the damaged workplace relations and to resist the systemic temptations that were built into the fabric of our jobs. Such is the life of the people of "The Other New York," whose lives are made to be vulnerable, stepping stones.

But the New York City Parking Meter Collectors achieved an important accomplishment, significant for the rest of their lives. Because in their example you will not have that normal, common tragedy of; "kicked in the butt," "felt like nothing," "got caught stealing," and the usual continuation of the choking, dying victim. Our journey took us off the beaten path, preserving and keeping intact our dignity and our importance as human beings, not allowing the theft of human spirit.

Contrary to what was going on among many of our city officials and the big business community, during the New York City corruption scandal, the Parking Meter Collectors emerged as a dedicated workforce, craving for the compassionate chemistry of the city, demonstrating respect for each other and for the public. Our collective sense of who we were went from "the guys that get the money out of the parking meters" to "the New York City Parking Meter Collectors. In this example, this workforce shares a precious experience together, amplifying what cooperation, trust and confidence really is. The pathway we took will reinforce the fiber of our families, as we maintain a very positive web of social relations among ourselves.

We are so very fortunate that New York City in our case, did not successfully achieve that assembly line production of manufacturing "broken people", because this is what normally happens in "The Other New York."

Wop-wop-wssh-waam!

Acknowledgements

Special thanks: to Nora Rivera, who many years ago tenaciously transcribed a number of recordings into a hard document, recognizing the value of this work. To Bob Wing who inspired me to complete this document, who transcribed and edited many recorded tapes early on, helping to solidify the foundation for telling this story. A very special appreciation to Kate Resto, my 1199 conductor, who was always available, even on little notice, to help this document evolve. To Jose Aponte, Raphael "Max" Medina, and Luis Cruz, who, as co-workers during the parking meter collector days, have created with me a formidable and lasting friendship, born out of struggle, bringing our families to share much love. Together we decided 30 years ago that this story was an important final assignment for me to complete, and they helped in documenting. Along with others, they hounded me over three decades to complete the task, and I am so deeply sorry that it has taken so long. Between family, work and simply finding my way, it often rested on the back burner. But hopefully it can still have an uplifting fulfillment to you and your families. I offer a very special thank you to Terry Schwadron, who has skillfully coached me to complete this work. I much appreciate what he has expertly brought to this effort. And finally, special appreciation to Minerva Solla, whose support, love and partnership have been so critical to this effort.

Initially we thought this experience would interest people, something that they needed to know about, that it would make for a good book or film. But as I have been working for many years with working people, I believe this experience is an important anomaly to what a workforce, or a department of employees, or a group of employees normally experience among themselves. Originally I had very little idea of what to emphasize about this journey until I had enough work experience as comparison. That body of experience to draw comparison too has turned out to be the last 30 years. Many everyday working people have been an inspiration to this document, sending chills up my spine. Through sticking together with their co-workers, they continued to teach me about the work experience, even in different parts of the world. Where we cross paths with divided workplaces, workers and employers have recognized that the employee relationship is precious, validating the real work that inspired these pages. I appreciate tremendously, the necessity of this story being within the context of working people being acknowledged, and achieving their rightful place in making social relations more successful.

Made in the USA
Lexington, KY
08 November 2015